ONE SEZ THIS THEN THE OTHER SEZ THAT

EXCERPTS FROM A WORK IN PROGRESS

by

David Halliwell

Hearing Eye

Published by **Hearing Eye**
99 Torriano Avenue
London
NW5 2RX

www.torriano.org

Printed at Catford Print Centre
Typeset by Daniel James at mondo designo
Copy Editor: Susan Johns

This publication has been made possible with the
financial assistance of Arts Council England

These excerpts from *One Sez This Then The Other Sez That*
were rehearsed at the Torriano Meeting House, Kentish
Town, and first performed at the Tristan Bates Theatre,
Covent Garden, on March 29th, 1999, with the following
cast:

Mike	Philip Ralph
Jane	Jill Howson
Director	David Halliwell
Assistant Director	Jane Clarke

Since these excerpts are from a work in progress, the
spelling of some words varies throughout the text.
Uniform orthography will be addressed during the
completion of the play.

ISBN 1 870841 90 5

ARTS COUNCIL ENGLAND

ONE SEZ THIS THEN THE OTHER SEZ THAT

An actor and actress walk onto the stage.

They bow to the audience.

They bow to each other.

They take up their positions for scene one.

Unless stated otherwise they move about the stage.

Wherever they happen to be at the end of a scene they pass immediately into the next scene.

Scene 1. Mike's Imagination.

MIKE: You're seriously misprised!
JANE: Am I?
MIKE: Yes.
JANE: What about when we went shopping?
MIKE: What about it?
JANE: Then you were seriously misprised.
MIKE: Was I?
JANE: You were.
MIKE: I didn't feel misprised.
JANE: You're always misprised.
MIKE: I'm never misprised.
JANE: Ah!
MIKE: What?
JANE: By saying that
MIKE: What?
JANE: You've just proved the opposite.
MIKE: Have I?
JANE: Yes.
MIKE: Well if I'm so misprised
JANE: Go on
MIKE: So mistaken
JANE: Go on
MIKE: Why did you want to buy a corn dolly?

JANE: For the house.
MIKE: Really?
JANE: To bring blessing and tranquillity to the house.
MIKE: Really?
JANE: Yes, to keep out evil spirits.
MIKE: Evil spirits?
JANE: Yes.
MIKE: Evil spirits.
JANE: Yes!

Pause.

Scene 2. Jane's Imagination.

MIKE: A lov' y'!
JANE: 'Ow d' y' meen?
MIKE: A meen A bluddy well lov' y'!
JANE: A don't know wot y'meen?
MIKE: A meen A bluddy well lov' y'!
JANE: A don't know wot y' talkin' about.
MIKE: A'm talkin' about lovin' y'.
JANE: I don't know wot
MIKE: D' y' 'ear wot A'm sayin'?
JANE: A don't know.
MIKE: D'y' fuckin' well 'ear wot A'm sayin?

Pause.

Scene 3. Mike's Imagination.

MIKE: The only evil spirits in this house
JANE: Yes?
MIKE: are your evil concoctions.
JANE: They're not evil.
MIKE: They're wicked.
JANE: They're beneficial
MIKE: For what?
JANE: For the whole of one's being.

MIKE: Oh the whole!
JANE: That's right.
MIKE: What about the part?
JANE: Part?
MIKE: Yes part. The only part of my being they reach is my bladder.
JANE: No
MIKE: Yes, and they don't stay there for very long.
JANE: Well that's because you don't drink them in the right frame of mind.
MIKE: If I drank them in the right frame of mind I wouldn't drink them at all.
JANE: Nonsense.
MIKE: Why'd you never want to buy anything practical?
JANE: Like a warehouse full of bin liners?
MIKE: They were going for a song.
JANE: The song didn't swing.
MIKE: But the bins do.
JANE: Who's
MIKE: The bins swung alright.
JANE: Who's talking about bins?
MIKE: I am.
JANE: Well I'm talking about liners.
MIKE: Er

Silence.

Scene 4. Jane's Imagination.

MIKE: D' y' fuckin well 'ear wot A'm sayin'!
JANE: S'pose so.
MIKE: Wot?
JANE: Well.
MIKE: Wot?
JANE: Well.
MIKE: Wot.
JANE: Well.

7

MIKE: Wot?
JANE: Well.
MIKE: Wot?
JANE: Well.
MIKE: Wot!

Pause.

JANE: Y' lov' me.
MIKE: Wot?
JANE: Y' lov' me.
MIKE: Right.

Pause.

Scene 5. Mike's Imagination.

JANE: I'm talking about liners!
MIKE: A life on the open wave.
JANE: If we'd bought the liners they'd've lasted us a
        thousand years.
MIKE: Oh no no no.
JANE: Oh yes.
MIKE: You exaggerate.
JANE: I don't think so.
MIKE: Oh yes.
JANE: No.
MIKE: More like fifty years!
JANE: We could've left them to our grandchildren.
MIKE: Haven't got any.
JANE: But if we had.
MIKE: What a delirious surprise for them.
JANE: Oh yes!
MIKE: Oh yes.
JANE: Go to bed a pauper, wake up a bin bag
        millionaire.
MIKE: Cry all the way to the dump
JANE: Oh you're so prosaic!

MIKE: I don't think so.
JANE: You have no sense of the mythopoeic!
MIKE: The what?

Pause.

Scene 6. Jane's Imagination.

JANE: Wot foh?
MIKE: 'Ow d' y' meen?
JANE: Wot d' y' lov' me foh?
MIKE: Wot do A lov' y' foh?
JANE: Aye wot d' y' lov' me foh?
MIKE: Don't y' know?
JANE: No.
MIKE: Y' do.
JANE: A don't.
MIKE: Y' do.
JANE: A don't.
MIKE: Y've no idea.
JANE: No.
MIKE: Non at all?
JANE: No.
MIKE: Y' 'ave.
JANE: A've not.
MIKE: Y' 'ave.
JANE: A've not.
MIKE: Well can't y'guess?
JANE: No.
MIKE: Not at all?
JANE: No

Silence.

Scene 7. Mike's Imagination.

JANE: The mythopoeic!
MIKE: Can't spell it.

9

JANE: All you can spell is dynorod.
MIKE: Yep, that's my kinda word.
JANE: Why d'you always argue about everything?
MIKE: Why d'you always argue about everything?
JANE: Snap!
MIKE: The voice of the pot.
JANE: The voice of the kettle.
MIKE: Well this is a kitchen.
JANE: How d'you know it's not an orangery?
MIKE: The colour of the walls.
JANE: Very funny.
MIKE: You simply do not know how to agree.
JANE: Nonsense.
MIKE: No, it was simply left out of your kit.
JANE: Oh no it wasn't
MIKE: Oh yes it was.
JANE: No, I am completely capable of concordance.
MIKE: Well if that is the case
JANE: And that is the case.
MIKE: then I am going to challenge you.
JANE: Challenge me?
MIKE: Yes, challenge you.
JANE: Er

Silence.

Scene 8. Jane's Imagination

MIKE: A lov' y' becos y' luvly.
JANE: Y' wot?
MIKE: Y' luvly.
JANE: Y' wot?
MIKE: Y' luvly.
JANE: Wot d' y' meen?
MIKE: A meen y' luvly.
JANE: Wot d' y' meen?
MIKE: A meen y' bluddy luvly.
JANE: 'Ow d' y' meen?

MIKE: Well

Silence.

Scene 9. Mike's Imagination.

JANE: Challenge me to what?
MIKE: To agree.
JANE: To agree?
MIKE: Yes.
JANE: How?
MIKE: I'll say something
JANE: Say what?
MIKE: and let's see whether you can agree.
JANE: Say what?
MIKE: Doesn't matter. Anything.
JANE: Anything?
MIKE: Yes.
JANE: You say anything?
MIKE: Yes.
JANE: And I'm supposed to agree?
MIKE: Yes.
JANE: Even if I don't agree?
MIKE: Yes. Just as an exercise.
JANE: Okay.
MIKE: You're on?
JANE: I'm on.
MIKE: But you won't be able to do it.
JANE: I will.
MIKE: No. You'll flunk it.

Silence.

Scene 10. Jane's Imagination.

MIKE: Y' luvly in y' appearance.
JANE: In me wot?
MIKE: In y' luks.

11

JANE: Me luks?
MIKE: Aye. Y' face.
JANE: Wot face?
MIKE: Y' face.
JANE: Me face?
MIKE: Aye y' face. Don't y' know wot y' face is?
JANE: 'Course a do.
MIKE: Well it's luvly.
JANE: No it in't.
MIKE: It is.
JANE: It in't.
MIKE: It is.
JANE: It in't.
MIKE: Why not?
JANE: A don't know.
MIKE: Well I know why it is.
JANE: Why?
MIKE: Becos it's oval.

Silence.

Scene 11. Mike's Imagination

JANE: I won't flunk it.
MIKE: You will.
JANE: Come on, come on, try me!
MIKE: Alright. Here goes. - We've just been shopping.
JANE: That is correct.
MIKE: Can I believe my ears?
JANE: Yes. Go on.
MIKE: We went into the grocer's.
JANE: We did.
MIKE: And in the grocer's we bumped into Miss
       Smith.
JANE: Well I wouldn't say bumped.
MIKE: Ah
JANE: I'd say accosted.
MIKE: Ah

JANE: I'd say she accosted us.
MIKE: Flunk!
JANE: Eh?
MIKE: Flunk, flunk, flunk!

Silence.

Scene 12. *Jane's Imagination*

JANE: It's not oval.
MIKE: It is.
JANE: No.
MIKE: Y' can't see it.
JANE: A've seen it.
MIKE: A'm starin' at it.
JANE: A've seen it.
MIKE: Well A'm sittin' 'ere starin' at it.
JANE: A c'n remember it.
MIKE: No y' can't.
JANE: 'Course A can.
MIKE: Y've forgotten it.
JANE: No A've not.
MIKE: Y'can't recall it.
JANE: You can't see straight.
MIKE: Well

Silence.

Scene 13. *Mike's Imagination*

MIKE: Flunk, flunk, flunk!
JANE: Oh! I'm sorry. A lapse. Continue.
MIKE: I will.
JANE: Yes, continue.
MIKE: But you won't be able to.
JANE: I will. Get on with it.
MIKE: Okay. Miss Smith told us a story.
JANE: She did.

MIKE: About something which happened a couple of days ago.

JANE: She did.

MIKE: Something which appears to be a bit of a mystery.

JANE: It does.

MIKE: She lives at the end of a hundred yard long cul-de-sac.

JANE: She does.

MIKE: Which runs at right angles to the main road.

JANE: It does.

MIKE: There are no other houses up the cul-de-sac.

JANE: There aren't.

MIKE: But there is one on the corner of the cul-de-sac and the main road.

JANE: There is.

MIKE: Inhabited by Mr. Robinson.

JANE: It is.

MIKE: And Mr. Robinson was in the shop alongside Miss Smith.

JANE: He was.

MIKE: Miss Smith told us that every morning a milk float delivers two bottles of milk to her door.

JANE: She did. But come on.

MIKE: Come on what?

JANE: What about you doing a spot of agreeing?

MIKE: Me?

JANE: Yes.

MIKE: Well

JANE: I've proved I can agree.

MIKE: Well

JANE: But can you?

MIKE: Well

Silence.

Scene 14. Jane's Imagination.

MIKE: A can see it's oval.
JANE: No.
MIKE: An' therefore luvly.
JANE: No.
MIKE: An' it's not t' on'y thing.
JANE: T' on'y wot?
MIKE: T' on'y thing.
JANE: T' on'y thing wot?
MIKE: S' not t' on'y thing 'at's luvly
JANE: Wot d'y' meen?
MIKE: Well y' figger.
JANE: Me wot?
MIKE: Y' figger.
JANE: 'Ow d' y' meen?
MIKE: Well

Silence.

Scene 15. Mike's Imagination.

JANE: Can you agree?
MIKE: I'm game!
JANE: Fine.
MIKE: Give me a whirl.
JANE: Coming up - A couple of mornings ago
MIKE: Yes.
JANE: on August the 15th to be exact
MIKE: Yes.
JANE: Miss Smith was in her kitchen.
MIKE: Yes
JANE: her kitchen faces the cul-de-sac
MIKE: Yes.
JANE: and nothing can come up or go down
MIKE: Yes.
JANE: without her being able to see it
MIKE: Yes.

JANE: on the morning of the 15th
MIKE: Yes.
JANE: she saw the milk float approaching
MIKE: Yes.
JANE: at the usual time
MIKE: Yes.
JANE: Just after 8 am
MIKE: Yes.
JANE: she saw the milkman get out of his cab
MIKE: Yes.
JANE: and advance towards her front door
MIKE: Yes.

Scene 16. Jane's Imagination.

MIKE: Well y' tits.
JANE: Wot tits?
MIKE: Your tits.
JANE: Y've never seen 'em.
MIKE: I 'ave.
JANE: Y' av'nt.
MIKE: A've seen where they are.
JANE: Where?
MIKE: There.
JANE: Where?
MIKE: On y'front, just below y'r arms.
JANE: Y' can't see 'em.
MIKE: A can.
JANE: Y' can't.
MIKE: 'Course A can.
JANE: They aren't visible.
MIKE: They are.
JANE: They aren't
MIKE: T' bulge is.
JANE: Wot bulge?
MIKE: T' bulge they make.
JANE: 'Ow d' y' know it's them.
MIKE: 'Ow do A know it's not?

Silence.

Scene 17. Mike's Imagination.

JANE: five minutes later
MIKE: Yes.
JANE: she opened the door
MIKE: looked down at her doorstep
JANE: and was surprised to find
MIKE: that although the empties had gone
JANE: there were no full bottles
MIKE: she exclaimed
JANE: 'where's my milk?'
MIKE: just as the postman
JANE: arrived with her mail
MIKE: and corroborated
JANE: there were no full bottles
MIKE: so she rang the dairy
JANE: to complain
MIKE: and the manager
JANE: promised to investigate
MIKE: which he did
JANE: and later in the morning
MIKE: he rang her
JANE: and reported that
MIKE: when the milkman
JANE: returned from his round
MIKE: he asked him
JANE: the milkman
MIKE: whether he'd delivered her milk
JANE: and the milkman said yes
MIKE: and indicated
JANE: as proof
MIKE: the complete absence of full bottles
JANE: on the float

Scene 18. Jane's Imagination.

JANE: 'Ow d y' know it's tits?
MIKE: Wot else cud it be?
JANE: 'O's t' say?
MIKE: It cudn't be owt else?
JANE: It cud.
MIKE: Wot?
JANE: A growth!
MIKE: A growth?
JANE: Cud be!
MIKE: Oh

Silence.

Scene 19. Mike's Imagination.

MIKE: yes but Robinson
JANE: Miss Smith's nearest neighbour
MIKE: who was standing right beside her
JANE: he didn't agree
MIKE: he didn't agree at all
JANE: he disputed what she'd told us
MIKE: he said he'd been working in his garden
JANE: when the milk float went by
MIKE: and he'd definitely seen
JANE: the milkman
MIKE: put two full bottles
JANE: onto her doorstep
MIKE: so there's a mystery
JANE: a conundrum
MIKE: Miss Smith and the postman
JANE: claim her milk wasn't delivered
MIKE: whilst the milkman the manager of the dairy and Robinson
JANE: claim that it was
MIKE: the case of the undelivered
JANE: or the delivered milk bottles

MIKE: yes
JANE: and there appears to be no explanation
MIKE: Oh I wouldn't say that
JANE: You wouldn't?
MIKE: No.

Scene 20. Jane's Imagination.

MIKE: No, it cudn't be a growth!
JANE: 'Ow d' you know?
MIKE: A know 'ow y'r' formed.
JANE: Y' don't.
MIKE: A do.
JANE: Y' don't.
MIKE: Y've tits up there.
JANE: Guesswork.
MIKE: An' a bum down below.
JANE: Y' wot?
MIKE: A bum.
JANE: A wot?
MIKE: A bum, a bottom, an arse.
JANE: 'Ow d'y' meen?
MIKE: Y can't deny y've got an arse!

Silence.

Scene 21. Mike's Imagination.

JANE: Then what would you say?
MIKE: There must be an explanation.
JANE: You think so?
MIKE: I do.
JANE: It can be explained?
MIKE: Yes.
JANE: You could explain it?
MIKE: I could.
JANE: Ha! I'd like to hear you try!
MIKE: Would you?

JANE: I would.
MIKE: Then your wish is about to come true.
JANE: Is it?
MIKE: It is.
JANE: Pray proceed.
MIKE: I'm about to.
JANE: Please do.

Scene 22. Jane's Imagination.

JANE: 'O's tryin'?
MIKE: So you'll admit that?
JANE: Wot?
MIKE: 'At y've got an arse?
JANE: S'pose so.
MIKE: An' it's luvly.
JANE: No.
MIKE: Y' wot?
JANE: It's not.
MIKE: It is! It's gorgeous.
JANE: Y' wot?
MIKE: Gorgeous!
JANE: It's not.
MIKE: It is.
JANE: Y've never seen it.
MIKE: 'Course I 'ave.
JANE: 'Ow?
MIKE: Thru' y' skirt.
JANE: 'Av' y' got X ray eyes?
MIKE: Course not.
JANE: Then 'ow 'v' y' seen it?
MIKE: Well

Silence.

Scene 23. Mike's Imagination.

MIKE: Try this - The milk was delivered!
JANE: Delivered?
MIKE: Yes the milkman delivered the milk.
JANE: Then what happened to it?
MIKE: It was stolen.
JANE: Stolen?
MIKE: Yeh.
JANE: By who?
MIKE: By whom!
JANE: By who!
MIKE: By whom!
JANE: Who stole it?
MIKE: Robinson.
JANE: Robinson?
MIKE: The nearest neighbour.
JANE: Why would he steal it?
MIKE: Revenge!
JANE: Revenge?
MIKE: Yes.
JANE: Revenge for what?
MIKE: Er

Silence.

Scene 24. Jane's Imagination.

MIKE: A'v' seen 'ow y'r arse displaces t' cloth.
JANE: That dun't mean owt.
MIKE: It duz.
JANE: It dun't.
MIKE: It meens A 'v' seen y'r arse.
JANE: No.
MIKE: An' it's gorgeous.
JANE: No.
MIKE: It's gorgeous.
JANE: It's nowt.

MIKE: It's magnificent.
JANE: It's plain.
MIKE: It's excitin'.
JANE: It's repulsive.
MIKE: It's fantastically excitin'!
JANE: No.
MIKE: It excites me.
JANE: 'Ow d' y' meen?
MIKE: A'm cummin thru me Y fronts.
JANE: Y'r on'y sayin' that becos it's Christmas.
MIKE: Christmas!
JANE: Aye.

Silence.

Scene 25. Mike's Imagination.

MIKE: Robinson had made a pass at Miss Smith.
JANE: You mean like in rugby?
MIKE: No. He wanted to screw her.
JANE: You mean make love?
MIKE: No, I mean bonk.
JANE: But she's hideous.
MIKE: So?
JANE: Built like a tank.
MIKE: So?
JANE: So why'd he want her?
MIKE: He's an old age pensioner.
JANE: Yes?
MIKE: She's single.
JANE: Yes?
MIKE: She's the best he could do.
JANE: Really?
MIKE: Or rather, not do.
JANE: Not do?
MIKE: Yes, she snubbed him. Humiliated him. He
        wanted revenge. He decided to start stealing
        her milk.

JANE: How'd that be revenge?
MIKE: Every morning he'd steal the milk. Every morning she'd complain. After a while the dairy'd get pissed off and stop delivering. She'd be seriously inconvenienced.
JANE: Oh come on, you've no evidence for that.
MIKE: Oh yes I have.
JANE: What?
MIKE: Er

Silence.

Scene 26. Jane's Imagination.

MIKE: It isn't Christmas.
JANE: It's November First.
MIKE: That's not Christmas.
JANE: Well it's neerly Christmas.
MIKE: Wot duz it matter?
JANE: It matters t' me..
MIKE: A'd say it any time.
JANE: Wot?
MIKE: At any time a' t' year.
JANE: Wot wud y' say?
MIKE: A lov' y'.
JANE: A don't know wot y' mean.
MIKE: Now listen y' stupid bugger.
JANE: A don't know wot y'r' on about.
MIKE: Listen y' stupid bugger.
JANE: A don't know wot
MIKE: Listen y' stupid fuckin' bugger!

Pause.

Scene 27. Mike's Imagination.

JANE: What evidence?
MIKE: What Robinson said.

JANE: What did he say?
MIKE: He was hoeing in his garden, he saw the milk float go by, go up the cul-de-sac and deliver Miss Smith's milk.
JANE: Well what's wrong with that?
MIKE: It's not plausible.
JANE: Sounds plausible to me.
MIKE: Listen carefully: for Robinson to have seen what he claims to have seen, he'd have to have stopped hoeing, gone over to his fence, and deliberately watched the float go up the cul-de-sac.
JANE: Well?
MIKE: Why should he claim that? To have deliberately observed such. a trivial everyday event? Something he could've seen a thousand times before? On that particular morning? Unless he's lying to give himself an alibi?

Silence.

Scene 28. Jane's Imagination.

MIKE: A fuckin' well lov' y'.
JANE: Well
MIKE: Wot do A do?
JANE: Well
MIKE: Wot do I do?
JANE: Y' lov'me.
MIKE: Right. Why?
JANE: A don't know.
MIKE: Y' wot?
JANE: A don't know.
MIKE: A've told y' becos y' luvly.
JANE: Y' wot?
MIKE: Becos y' bluddy well luvly.
JANE: No A'm not.
MIKE: You bluddy well are.

24

JANE: No A'm not.
MIKE: You fuckin' well are.
JANE: No.
MIKE: Now listen!
JANE: No.
MIKE: Listen t' me!
JANE: No.
MIKE: Listen y' thick bugger!
JANE: No.
MIKE: Listen or A'll nock y' teeth in!
JANE: Well
MIKE: A'll nock y' mis'rable teeth in!
JANE: Well
MIKE: A'll nock 'em down y' mawngy throat!
JANE: Well
MIKE: Listen y' rancid bitch!
JANE: Well
MIKE: Listen y' foul fuckin' cunt!
JANE: Well
MIKE: Listen y' stinkin' lumpa shit! Y'r luvly!

Silence.

Scene 29. Mike's Imagination.

JANE: Alright, suppose he did steal the milk on
        August 15th, why hasn't he stolen it since?
MIKE: Easy!
JANE: Easy?
MIKE: Yes
JANE: Why?
MIKE: Miss Smith's big mouth.
JANE: Big mouth?
MIKE: Yes, she's been yapping.
JANE: So?
MIKE: Telling all and sundry about her bottles.
JANE: And?
MIKE: He's lost his bottle. It's frightened him off.

JANE: So he only stole the milk once?
MIKE: Yes.
JANE: Well how did he manage it without being seen
        by Miss Smith?

Silence.

Scene 30. Jane's Imagination.

JANE: Well, even if I am luvly, wot about t' other nite?
MIKE: What y' talkin' about?
JANE: Y' know very well what A'm talkin' about.
MIKE: A most certainly
JANE: Oh, yes, y' do.
MIKE: A don't.
JANE: You know.
MIKE: I 'av'n't the faintest
JANE: Oh, don't come
MIKE: Now look
JANE: You look.
MIKE: Me look?
JANE: Yes, you.
MIKE: Why should A?
JANE: Oh, aye, why should y'?
MIKE: Yes. Why?
JANE: Y' know very well.
MIKE: A don't.
JANE: Y' do.
MIKE: All right if I know
JANE: You know
MIKE: Then what is it?
JANE: What's what?
MIKE: What is it?

Pause.

Scene 31. Mike's Imagination.

JANE: How did he manage without being seen by
        Miss Smith?
MIKE: No problem.
JANE: No problem?
MIKE: No, he ran.
JANE: Did you say ran?
MIKE: Yes.
JANE: Ran?
MIKE: Yes.
JANE: Are you sure you want to say ran?
MIKE: Of course I am.
JANE: But he only had five minutes to cover 200
        yards, up to Miss Smith's and down again.
        Between when you say the milk was delivered
        and when Miss Smith opened her door.
MIKE: So what?
JANE: So what?
MIKE: Yes. if people can run a mile in less than three
        minutes why couldn't Robinson run a mere 200
        yards in five?
JANE: I'll tell you.
MIKE: Yes?
JANE: He has a slight problem.
MIKE: What's that?
JANE: He can't run.
MIKE: Oh no.
JANE: He's old.
MIKE: No.
JANE: He's stiff.
MIKE: No.
JANE: He's arthritic.
MIKE: No.
JANE: He's paralysed.
MIKE: No.
JANE: Alright, I exaggerate, he's not paralysed - he
        can move his left thumb.

MIKE: Don't be facetious.
JANE: I'm being facetious?
MIKE: Yes.
JANE: You've got to admit he's got arthritis.
MIKE: Very mildly.
JANE: You exaggerate.
MIKE: If Robinson's as arthritic as you say, how come he can keep up his enormous garden?
JANE: Well

Silence.

Scene 32. Jane's Imagination.

JANE: If y' know A don't need t'tell y'.
MIKE: A don't know.
JANE: Y' said y' did.
MIKE: When?
JANE: Just now.
MIKE: A didn't.
JANE: Y' did.
MIKE: A said now't a't' sort.
JANE: Then what did y' say?
MIKE: When?
JANE: Just now.
MIKE: A didn't say anything.
JANE: Y' did.
MIKE: A didn't.
JANE: Y' did.
MIKE: What did A say?
JANE: Y' said y' did.
MIKE: Did what?

Pause.

Scene 33. Mike's Imagination.

MIKE: He works on it morning, noon and night.

JANE: Well

MIKE: We've seen him.

JANE: Well it doesn't matter how quickly he can or can't run, he couldn't have stolen Miss Smith's milk without being seen.

MIKE: Ah

JANE: She was in her kitchen

MIKE: Ah

JANE: with a clear view all the way down the cul-de-sac

MIKE: Ah

JANE: however fast he could run she'd have seen him.

MIKE: I didn't say he ran up the cul-de-sac!

JANE: Well where did he run?

MIKE: Up the field which borders the cul-de-sac. It's hidden from Miss Smith's view by a hedge. Robinson ran up the field, climbed through the hedge and crawled on his hands and knees to Miss Smith's door from the side. Below her line of vision!

JANE: Crawled?

MIKE: Yes.

JANE: But that would involve crawling several yards.

MIKE: So?

JANE: He couldn't have done it in the time.

MIKE: Course he could.

JANE: Not in addition to running up the field and climbing through the hedge.

MIKE: Course he could.

JANE: No. Crawling on your hands and knees would be extremely painful. There'd be tremendous pressure on the joints. For an old man like Robinson with arthritis it'd be excruciating. He'd only be able to move at snail pace.

MIKE: Well

Silence.

Scene 34. Jane's Imagination.

JANE: Y'sed y'did know.
MIKE: A didn't.
JANE: Then what?
MIKE: A said
JANE: Don't
MIKE: I said
JANE: Look don't
MIKE: Let me finish.
JANE: 'O's stoppin' y?
MIKE: You are.
JANE: A'm not.
MIKE: You are.
JANE: Go on, go on.
MIKE: All right.
JANE: Go ahead.
MIKE: A will.
JANE: Do.
MIKE: Right, A said A didn't.
JANE: What
MIKE: I said I did not.

Silence.

Scene 35. Mike's Imagination.

MIKE: Well - he didn't crawl, he slithered!
JANE: Slithered?
MIKE: Yes, not like a snail but like a snake, with his belly on the ground, y' know, swiftly from side to side.
JANE: Nobody could do that.
MIKE: Course they could. There's no pressure on the hands and knees.
JANE: No human being can slither.
MIKE: Course they can, it's quick, smooth and easy.
JANE: Quick smooth and easy?

MIKE: Yes, you just wiggle from side to side.
JANE: Alright, let's see you do it.
MIKE: Me?
JANE: Yes you.
MIKE: Well I can't do it here.
JANE: Why not?
MIKE: There's a carpet here.
JANE: So what?
MIKE: The friction with the pile would get in the way.
JANE: Nonsense. And it's not a carpet anyway.
MIKE: What is it?
JANE: A mat.
MIKE: Well the friction from the fibres would get in the way.
JANE: Nonsense.
MIKE: Static electricity would impede the flow.
JANE: Nonsense.
MIKE: It'd be quite different on a pavement.
JANE: Nonsense. It should be easier on a smooth, level mat than on a rough, uneven pavement.

Silence.

Scene 36. Jane's Imagination.

JANE: Don't talk like that.
MIKE: Fuh...!
JANE: Didn't what?
MIKE: Don't tell me...! Y' know very well.
JANE: Very well what?
MIKE: Y' know.
JANE: A don't.
MIKE: Oh, so y' admit it.
JANE: Admit?
MIKE: Yes, admit it.
JANE: Admit what?
MIKE: Admit y' don't know.
JANE: A don't admit anything.

MIKE: Oh, yes, y' did.
JANE: What?
MIKE: That y' don't know what y're talkin' about.
JANE: Oh, no. A don't.
MIKE: That's what A'm saying.
JANE: Sayin' what?
MIKE: That y' don't know.

Silence.

Scene 37. Mike's Imagination

MIKE: Alright - Robinson didn't slither.
JANE: You amaze me.
MIKE: He approached the house directly.
JANE: Directly?
MIKE: Yes. Up the cul-de-sac.
JANE: But he'd've been seen.
MIKE: He was seen.
JANE: Was seen?
MIKE: Yes. He drove up in the milk float!
JANE: The milk float?
MIKE: Yes. He waved the milk float down just before it
        entered the cul-de-sac, persuaded the milkman
        to let him deliver Miss Smith's milk, he donned
        the milkman's coat and cap and didn't deliver
        her milk.
JANE: He stole her milk by not delivering it?
MIKE: Precisely. He stole by omission.
JANE: Well how did he persuade the milkman to let
        him use the float?
MIKE: He bribed him.
JANE: Bribed him?
MIKE: Yes.
JANE: But Robinson's an old age pensioner.
MIKE: Well
JANE: Without two pee to rub together. You can tell

from his clothes, from the state of his cottage.
MIKE: Well

Silence.

Scene 38. Jane's Imagination.

JANE: I know all right.
MIKE: Y' just said y' didn't.
JANE: A know only too well.
MIKE: Then why d' y' say y' didn't?
JANE: A didn't.
MIKE: Y' did.
JANE: A said A didn't say A didn't A didn't say A
        didn't know.
MIKE: Y' didn't say y' didn't say y' didn't!
JANE: A didn't say A didn't know.
MIKE: Y' don't know what y' said.
JANE: Of course A do.
MIKE: Then what was it?
JANE: Oh, yes, try t' switch it on t' me.
MIKE: A'm not tryin'.
JANE: As usual.
MIKE: What a' y' talkin'
JANE: Your usual trick.
MIKE: What trick?
JANE: Switch the blame.

Pause.

Scene 39. Mike's Imagination.

JANE: What did he bribe the milkman with?
MIKE: Well
JANE: A colander full of used tea bags?
MIKE: No.
JANE: A loan of his false teeth?
MIKE: No.

JANE: His body? A night of romance in the ambience of the compost heap?

MIKE: No!

JANE: Why don't you claim he hijacked the float?

MIKE: Oh

JANE: Knocked the milkman out with a cucumber?

MIKE: Oh now

JANE: Undelivered the milk.

MIKE: Oh now

JANE: Then revived the milkman with fermented beetroot juice.

MIKE: Oh now, cut that out!

JANE: Cut what out?

MIKE: Making with the cracks.

JANE: Cracks?

MIKE: Yes.

JANE: My cracks only point out the cracks in your explanation.

MIKE: There aren't any cracks!

JANE: Oh no!

MIKE: No.

JANE: Then explain to me; how did Robinson steal the milk?

MIKE: Well

Silence.

Scene 40. Jane's Imagination.

MIKE: It's no trick - you started it.

JANE: I started it?

MIKE: Yes, you started it by

JANE: 'Ow could I start it?

MIKE: Y' said

JANE: A'm not talkin' about what I said

MIKE: Well

JANE: A'm talkin' about what you did.

MIKE: A don't know what

JANE: Oh, stop being so... coy.
MIKE: Coy?
JANE: Yes, coy.
MIKE: Coy! Y' think this is bein' coy?
JANE: Oh, stop
MIKE: Y' don't know the meanin' of words.
JANE: A know what you're up to.
MIKE: Up to?
JANE: Yes, cut it out.
MIKE: A'm simply

Silence.

Scene 41. Mike's Imagination.

MIKE: Well - he stole it from above rather than below.
JANE: From above?
MIKE: Yes.
JANE: And how did he accomplish that?
MIKE: By balloon!
JANE: Balloon?
MIKE: That's right.
JANE: You mean a kiddie's coloured balloon?
MIKE: Don't be silly. I mean a proper balloon which carries people. With a basket, an engine and a propeller. I mean a dirigible.
JANE: A dirigible?
MIKE: That's right.
JANE: How would Robinson come by a dirigible?
MIKE: Bought it.
JANE: Oh come on, he couldn't afford a kiddie's balloon, never mind a dirigible.
MIKE: He bought it years ago. When he had money.
JANE: But why the hell should he buy a dirigible?
MIKE: Lotsa people buy dirigibles.
JANE: Oh yes, as y'do, I pick up one every time I go to the supermarket.
MIKE: Practical people, sporting people, they fly about

in them for fun.
JANE: So Robinson bought a dirigible for fun?
MIKE: Certainly.
JANE: Then why did nobody see him in it?
MIKE: Well

Silence.

Scene 42. Jane's Imagination.

JANE: We've 'eard it all before.
MIKE: A'm just trying t' find out what y'r' talkin'
       about.
JANE   It doesn't work.
MIKE: What a' y'
JANE: Y' know very well.
MIKE: All right you tell me.
JANE: Tell y'!
MIKE: Yes, you tell me.
JANE: Tell y' what?
MIKE: What y' mean.
JANE: Oh
MIKE: Y' can't.
JANE: Oh can't A?
MIKE: No, y' can't.
JANE: Y' think A can't.
MIKE: A do.
JANE: You're so
MIKE: Go on tell me.

Silence.

Scene 43. Mike's Imagination.

MIKE: He only flew at night.
JANE: Why should he only fly at night?
MIKE: He preferred it.
JANE: Why did he prefer it?

MIKE: There are no birds about at night.
JANE: What does that mean?
MIKE: He didn't want to bump into one.
JANE: What about owls?
MIKE: They hoot so you know where they are.
JANE: Oh come off it, if Robinson had bought a
balloon the whole town would've known about
it.
MIKE: No, he never talked about it.
JANE: Why not?
MIKE: Nobody ever asked him.
JANE: Oh listen, if you've got a balloon you're going
to want to talk about it.
MIKE: Not Robinson.
JANE: Why not?
MIKE: He didn't want to be a laughing stock.
JANE: Why should he be a laughing stock?
MIKE: Suppose he'd had a crash, you know what
small town gossips are like.
JANE: But somebody must've seen it.
MIKE: No.
JANE: I mean when it was delivered to his cottage.
MIKE: It was delivered in the dark.
JANE: And he's been wafting about in the dark ever
since?
MIKE: No.
JANE: How come?
MIKE: He only went up a couple of times.
JANE: Why's that?
MIKE: Er

Silence.

Scene 44. Jane's Imagination.

JANE: Why should A tell y'?
MIKE: Y' can't.
JANE: A can.

MIKE: Go on then.
JANE: All right.
MIKE: Go on.
JANE: A will.
MIKE: Fine.
JANE: A will don't worry.
MIKE: Right, go on.
JANE: Don't worry.
MIKE: A'm all ears.
JANE: All right. You refused.
MIKE: Refused.
JANE: A knew y' wouldn't accept it.

Silence.

Scene 45. Mike's Imagination.

MIKE: He didn't like ballooning.
JANE: Didn't like it?
MIKE: No.
JANE: Why not?
MIKE. He found it boring.
JANE: Boring?
MIKE: Yes. Floating about at night; there's nothing to see.
JANE: So why didn't he sell the balloon?
MIKE: He couldn't.
JANE: Why?
MIKE: Nobody wanted to buy it.
JANE: Why?
MIKE: The market had become deflated.
JANE: Like your arguments.
MIKE: My arguments aren't deflated.
JANE: No, they're inflated.
MIKE: How can they be both deflated and inflated?
JANE: It's Zen.
MIKE: It's zany.
JANE: So Robinson kept his balloon?

MIKE: Yes.
JANE: But come on, balloons are enormous things.
MIKE: Not when they're deflated.
JANE: Oh yes, even then.
MIKE: No, the bag would fit into a box the size of a tea chest.
JANE: What about the basket and the engine?
MIKE: The size of a small car. The whole lot would fit easily into the back of the average garage.
JANE: Robinson hasn't got a garage.
MIKE: Er

Silence.

Scene 46. Jane's Imagination.

MIKE: That's crap.
JANE: Go on deny it.
MIKE: A've no intention of
JANE: Y' can't.
MIKE: There's nothing t' deny.
JANE: Are y' tryin' to mek out y' didn't refuse?
MIKE: No, A'm not.
JANE: Wonders'll never cease.
MIKE: A'm sayin' 'e never offered.
JANE: 'E?
MIKE: Aye.
JANE: 'O?

Pause.

Scene 47. Mike's Imagination.

MIKE: He has a shed in his garden.
JANE: A tool shed.
MIKE: Robinson's balloon is a very small model. Designed to carry only one person.
JANE: And where did he inflate it to make his epic

flight?

MIKE: Behind his house where nobody could see.

JANE: Then what?

MIKE: He got into the basket, started the engine, and rose into the air.

JANE: And nobody saw him rise.

MIKE: The back of his house is screened by tall trees.

JANE: Go on.

MIKE: He flew to Miss Smith's house by a circuitous route and approached the house from behind.

JANE: And nobody saw him fly?

MIKE: Nobody looked up.

JANE: But if they had looked up.

MIKE: But they didn't.

JANE: But what about the engine?

MIKE: What about the engine?

JANE: It must've made a noise.

MIKE: He flew high, it couldn't be heard from the ground.

JANE: And when he reached Miss Smith's?

MIKE: He switched the engine off.

JANE: And then what?

MIKE: He descended over the house.

JANE: He must've cast a huge shadow.

MIKE: Miss Smith thought it was a cloud.

JANE: She never mentioned a cloud.

MIKE: Who mentions clouds?

JANE: So how did he steal the milk?

MIKE: He hovered over the house. He lowered a line. A very fine line, almost invisible but very strong. He lassoed each milk bottle and whizzed it aloft.

JANE: Lassoed each milk bottle?

MIKE: Yes.

JANE: Impossible.

MIKE: Why?

Silence.

Scene 48. Jane's Imagination.

MIKE: Well, they then, they
JANE: Y' said 'e.
MIKE: What duz it matter?
JANE: 'O d' y' mean?
MIKE: Oh, A'm not goin' mention anybody in partic'lar. It duzn't matter.
JANE: Oh, yes, it duz.
MIKE: It doesn't.
JANE: It means you admit somebody did offer.
MIKE: A said 'e didn't.
JANE: 'O?
MIKE: Oh, y' know.
JANE: A don't.

Silence.

Scene 49. Mike's Imagination.

JANE: His balloon would be moving.
MIKE: No it was static.
JANE: It can't have been static.
MIKE: As I've said, he'd turned off the engine.
JANE: Make no difference.
MIKE: He'd thrown down an anchor.
JANE: Make no difference.
MIKE: How can you say that?
JANE: Balloons can't remain static. They can't hover. They bobble and wobble about, they rise and fall, they sway from side to side, pushed by the wind, disturbed by air currents. Lassoing milk bottles from a rapidly moving balloon would be vastly more difficult than being drunk and threading a needle in a raging blizzard on the heaving rolling deck of a capsizing ship that's sinking fast!

Silence.

Scene 50. Jane's Imagination.

MIKE: Guess o' it was.
JANE: Luvly legs?
MIKE: Ron.
JANE: Yes. Mr. Tripod 'imself.
MIKE: Don't call 'im that.
JANE: Oh no, y' don't like that.
MIKE: Now don't start on that.
JANE: Oh no, we musn't start on that.
MIKE: You always bring things back to that.
JANE: Well, that's a very important subj
MIKE: We aren't discussin' that.
JANE: We musn't even discuss it.
MIKE: We were discussin'
JANE: Ron an' 'is
MIKE: We weren't discussin' Ron in that connection. Now y' know... That's it. No more. T' only point about Ron A'm prepared to discuss is whether or not 'e offered.
JANE: 'E

Pause.

Scene 51. Mike's Imagination.

JANE: Aha! You can't answer!
MIKE: How d'you know I can't answer?
JANE: Because if you could answer you would.
MIKE: Well at least I came up with an explanation.
JANE: Meaning?
MIKE: It's more than you could do.
JANE: You think so?
MIKE: I do.
JANE: Then I'll disabuse you.

MIKE:	Disabuse me?
JANE:	Yes.
MIKE:	I'd love to see you try.
JANE:	Here I go!
MIKE:	I don't think so!

Scene 52. Jane's Imagination.

MIKE:	'E never showed t' slightest indication of offerin'
JANE:	Then why did y' single 'im out then?
MIKE:	A didn't single 'im out.
JANE:	Then why d' y' bring 'im up?
MIKE:	Oh, I dunno... becos A knew you'd try t' mek out 'e 'ad.
JANE:	Why should
MIKE:	It's always Ron this and Ron that.
JANE:	A never said a word about 'im.
MIKE:	Just becos 'e flashes
JANE:	A thought we weren't talkin' about
MIKE:	A'm not talkin' about that, A'm talkin' about t'way 'e parades 'imself, 'is money - not 'at 'e 'as any - an' 'is so called wit

Pause.

Scene 53. Mike's Imagination.

JANE:	The milkman didn't deliver the milk!
MIKE:	Are you saying he's lying?
JANE:	No. he's not lying.
MIKE:	Then what d'you mean?
JANE:	His motivation was completely unconscious.
MIKE:	Unconscious?
JANE:	Yes. The milkman's mother never breastfed him. He felt deprived of her milk. He felt resentful and wanted to punish her. But he had to wait until he was in his teens before he could

do anything about it. Then his mother fell ill and he was supposed to look after her. But he neglected her - thus symbolically depriving her of milk - and she died. Then, to compensate for having killed her, he took over her role, he became her, or rather became what she should've been. He became a dispenser of milk, he became a milkman. Everything went smoothly until the conjunction of two fifteens: August 15th and the number of Miss Smith's house, number 15. Even though it's at the end of the cul-de-sac it's numbered as though it's on the main road. This conjunction reminded the milkman of an earlier conjunction: his mother died on August 15th when he was fifteen. This triggered a regression and he felt a powerful urge to symbolically re-enact what had happened then. On August 15th he wanted to deprive the woman in number 15 of her milk.

Silence.

Scene 54. Jane's Imagination

JANE: Well, you just sat there.
MIKE: A did not.
JANE: At least Ron kept things goin'.
MIKE: Oh, aye, 'e kept t'coffee goin', comin' an' goin', coffee, coffee, coffee, some of 'em Gaelic!
JANE: No.
MIKE: One of 'em was.
JANE: Well, a few coffees, what's
MIKE: Nine, 'e 'ad nine.
JANE: Some 'ost you are countin' t' coffees.
MIKE: A minute ago y' were criticizin' me for payin'.
JANE: Not for a few coffees.
MIKE: Oh, that's your idea of invitin' a few friends out for a meal, is it?

44

JANE: No A

Silence.

Scene 55. Mike's Imagination.

MIKE: And all that was unconscious?
JANE: Completely unconscious.
MIKE: And how can you know all that?
JANE: I know.
MIKE: You've only spoken to the milkman once.
JANE: Doesn't matter.
MIKE: And then only for two minutes.
JANE: It was enough. I could tell.
MIKE: How could you tell?
JANE: I have ways of telling.
MIKE: Then tell me.
JANE: One has a certain subliminal perception.
MIKE: Ah subliminal perception!
JANE: An extrasensory insight.
MIKE: Ah extrasensory insight!
JANE: Yes.
MIKE: Where'd you keep 'em?
JANE: Eh

Silence.

Scene 56. Jane's Imagination.

MIKE: They pay for their own food but y' buy 'em a
        coffee t'wash it down with.
JANE: Friends! Y' call that gang friends.
MIKE: They are my friends.
JANE: So Ron's a friend now?
MIKE: No, not Ron but
JANE: Then why invite 'im?
MIKE: Oh, 'e was just a makeweight but t' rest
JANE: Maxwell! Binnie an' Bennie! Jean whatser

MIKE: Yes, they are.
JANE: A can never tell which is Binnie an' which is
Bennie.
MIKE: Y' know very well which is
JANE: All out for what they can grab, that's all.
MIKE: Oh, 'ow is it then they were all clamourin'
t'pay?
JANE: They weren't.
MIKE: Y' said they were.
JANE: A said some offered, some, an' you refused.
MIKE: 'O offered?
JANE: What about Maxwell?
MIKE: Maxwell's never paid 'is whack in 'is life.
JANE: 'E got out 'is wallet.
MIKE: 'E didn't.
JANE: A saw 'im.
MIKE: E moved 'is 'and inside 'is jacket that's all,
momentarily, just like this, a fleetin' movement,
that's all 'e ever duz.
JANE: Oh no.
MIKE: It wasn't in there above a second in fact it never
really went in at all.
JANE: A've just seen what you did an' A never
thought you'd tekken out y'r wallet.

Silence.

Scene 57. Mike's Imagination.

JANE: Haven't' you heard of vibes?
MIKE: Yeh, they're a musical instrument.
JANE: Oh don't be facetious.
MIKE: Why don't you claim the milkman's dad was a
jazz musician
JANE: Don't be
MIKE: who played black music
JANE: Don't be
MIKE: causing the son to become a milkman

46

JANE: Don't be
MIKE: dispensing white liquid in revenge?
JANE: Don't be ridiculous!
MIKE: Who's being ridiculous?
JANE: You are.
MIKE: I'm being ridiculous?
JANE: Of course you are.
MIKE: Well, if you're being serious
JANE: I am.
MIKE: what about all the previous years?
JANE: What about all the previous years?
MIKE: All the previous years the milkman's been doing the same round. Why didn't he deprive Miss Smith of her milk every August 15th?

Silence.

Scene 58. Jane's Imagination.

MIKE: 'E's a lot cleverer at pretendin t' tek out 'is wallet 'an I am.
JANE: Any excuse.
MIKE: 'E duz'nt even 'ave a wallet in there.
JANE: 'Ow d'you know?
MIKE: A know where 'e keeps 'is money, A've known 'im for years an' A've been all over with 'im, 'e keeps it in 'is back pocket with a button always buttoned up.
JANE: Then if 'e's so mean why lavish a meal on 'im?
MIKE: Well

Silence.

Scene 59. Mike's Imagination.

JANE: Because he was waiting.
MIKE: Waiting?
JANE: Yes.

MIKE: Waiting for what?

JANE: The anniversary.

MIKE: Anniversary of what?

JANE: His mother's death.

MIKE: His mother's death?

JANE: Yes, the fifteenth anniversary of his mother's death.

MIKE: Oh come on.

JANE: This year wasn't simply a double conjunction

MIKE: Do me a favour.

JANE: It was a triple conjunction!

MIKE: Please!

JANE: Yes a symbolic reversion to the original event which took place half his life ago. The end of a cycle. He'll do it again in fifteen years' time.

MIKE: I can hardly wait.

JANE: Don't be

MIKE: Why not make it a sextuple conjunction?

JANE: How d'you mean?

MIKE: Why not say he was wearing size fifteen shoes, had fifteen teeth in his mouth, and a fifteen inch prick in his trousers?

JANE: Because that would be nonsense.

MIKE: That would be nonsense!

JANE: Three mornings ago the milkman unconsciously decided not to deliver milk to Miss Smith!

MIKE: Oh, of course, unconsciously.

JANE: Of course.

MIKE: I mean does this guy ever do anything consciously?

JANE: Of course he does.

MIKE: I'm surprised he finds time.

JANE: He does both at the same time.

MIKE: Really?

JANE: Yes.

MIKE: So why does this guy go all the way up the cul-de-sac not to deliver milk?

Silence.

Scene 60. Jane's Imagination.

JANE: If they're all so tight why
MIKE: A didn't say they were all
JANE: If none of 'em offered.
MIKE: A didn't say none of 'em offered.
JANE: Oh yes, y' did.
MIKE: Now luk it was you.
JANE: It wasn't.
MIKE: Y' never stick t'
JANE: It's you 'o duzn't stick.
MIKE: 'Ow d' y' mek that out?
JANE: Y' know very well.
MIKE: A don't know what y're talkin' about.
JANE: Oh, yes, y' do.
MIKE: A don't.
JANE: 'Course y' do.
MIKE: A don't.
JANE: Y' do.
MIKE: What a' y'

Silence.

Scene 61. Mike's Imagination.

JANE: The milkman goes all the way up the cul-de-sac
        to maintain his conscious perception that he
        was going to deliver the milk until the moment
        arrived when he didn't deliver the milk. Then
        when he hadn't delivered the milk he had to
        maintain the perception that he had delivered
        the milk.
MIKE: Thanks for making everything clear.
JANE: It's obvious.
MIKE: So what happened at the moment he didn't

deliver the milk?

JANE: When he got to the house he stopped the float and went into a trance. He remained motionless in the cab but he consciously experienced getting out of the cab, taking two bottles from a crate, walking to the doorstep and leaving them there.

MIKE: He remained completely immobile?

JANE: Yes.

MIKE: So what did Miss Smith see?

JANE: Er

Silence.

Scene 62. Jane's Imagination.

MIKE: Listen, never mind 'o offered. I 'avn't 'ad a shit f'five days.

JANE: Eh?

MIKE: I 'avn't 'ad a shit f'five days.

JANE: A wot?

MIKE: A shit.

JANE: A shit?

MIKE: Aye a shit.

JANE: Y' av'.

MIKE: 'Av' not.

JANE: Y' av'.

MIKE: I 'avn't

JANE: Y' 'd one yesterday.

MIKE: A didn't

JANE: Y' did

MIKE: A didn't

JANE: Y' did

MIKE: A didn't

JANE: Y' did

MIKE: When?

JANE: When wot?

MIKE: When yesterday?

JANE: T' evenin'
MIKE: No
JANE: About eight thirty-five.
MIKE: No.
JANE: Y'did
MIKE: Never
JANE: Y'did
MIKE: 'Ow d 'y' know?
JANE: 'Ow d' y' think?
MIKE: 'Ow shud I know?

Silence.

Scene 63. Mike's Imagination

JANE: His astral body.
MIKE: His astral body?
JANE: His spiritual body.
MIKE: His spiritual body?
JANE: Yes, he projected his spiritual body so that it
        appeared to deliver the milk.
MIKE: But it didn't really deliver the milk?
JANE: Of course not.
MIKE: But it did really collect the empties?
JANE: Yes.
MIKE: That was very clever of it.
JANE: What's the difference between real and unreal?
MIKE: What I say's real. What you say's unreal.
JANE: The other way round.
MIKE: So what happened when the milkman got back
        to the dairy? He still had two full bottles on his
        float.
JANE: Well

Silence.

Scene 64. Jane's Imagination.

MIKE: 'Ow shud I know?
JANE: A saw y'
MIKE: Saw me?
JANE: Yes.
MIKE: 'Avin' a shit?
JANE: Yes.
MIKE: Where?
JANE: Don't y' know?
MIKE: Where did this alleged event tek place?
JANE: Where d' y' think?
MIKE: In your Imagination.
JANE: No.
MIKE: Then where?
JANE: In t' lav.
MIKE: Wot lav?
JANE: Our lav.
MIKE: 'O's lav?
JANE: Ours
MIKE: 'O's?
JANE: Ours
MIKE: Ours?
JANE: Aye. T' lav at our 'ouse
MIKE: Wot lav at our 'ouse?
JANE: At t' top a' t' stairs
MIKE: At t' top a' wot stairs?
JANE: On t'left
MIKE: The's no lav on t'left.
JANE: There is
MIKE: There isn't.
JANE: A'm talkin' about our 'ouse.
MIKE: So am I.
JANE: About t' top a' t' stairs.
MIKE: So am I.
JANE: About t' lav t' t' left.
MIKE: The's no lav t' t' left.
JANE: 'Course there is.
MIKE: The's one t' t' right.
JANE: There isn't

MIKE: There is.
JANE: The's not.
MIKE: I know where our lav is.
JANE: Y' don't seem to.
MIKE: A know very well
JANE: Y've a funny way a' showin' it.
MIKE: An' A didn't use it yesterday.
JANE: Y' did.
MIKE: 'Ow d' y' know?

Silence.

Scene 65. Mike's Imagination.

JANE: Well - he didn't take the bottles back to the
        dairy.
MIKE: He didn't?
JANE: No. He noticed them just before he got back.
MIKE: And?
JANE: He remembered he hadn't delivered them to
        Miss Smith.
MIKE: He remembered?
JANE: Yes.
MIKE: How the hell could he remember not delivering
        milk when you say he's psyched himself into
        believing he had delivered milk?
JANE: The memory that he hadn't was in his
        unconscious. When he spotted the full bottles it
        leapt into his conscious mind.
MIKE: Why did it do that?
JANE: Because now he needed it.
MIKE: Why?
JANE: Because he unconsciously realised that if he
        took the full bottles back to the dairy he'd have
        to admit he hadn't delivered them.
MIKE: And why did he think he hadn't delivered
        them?
JANE: Absent mindedness.

MIKE: You can say that again.
JANE: It'd slipped his mind.
MIKE: So what did he do?
JANE: Delivered them to Miss Smith.
MIKE: Delivered them to Miss Smith?
JANE: Yes.
MIKE: After he'd undelivered them he delivered them?
JANE: Yes.
MIKE: But he'd have to go all the way back to her house. He'd be late back at the dairy.
JANE: Er

Silence.

Scene 66. Jane's Imagination.

JANE: A saw y'.
MIKE: Saw me?
JANE: Saw y'.
MIKE: Saw me wot?
JANE: Saw y' goin' in.
MIKE: Saw me goin' in?
JANE: Saw y' goin' in.
MIKE: Wot duz that prove?
JANE: Wot d' y' meen?
MIKE: It proves A went in.
JANE: Y' did.
MIKE: But it dun't prove A did owt once inside.
JANE: 'Course it duz.
MIKE: No it dun't
JANE: A know you of old
MIKE: Y' don't.
JANE: A know wot you get up to in there
MIKE: Y' don't
JANE: A do.
MIKE: No.
JANE: A do.

54

MIKE: Wot?
JANE: Wot wot?
MIKE: Wot did A do in there?
JANE: In where?
MIKE: In t' lav
JANE: Y' ad a shit.
MIKE: No.
JANE: Y' ad a wee wee
MIKE: I did not 'ave a wee wee.
JANE: Y' did 'ave a wee wee.
MIKE: Pure speculation
JANE: An' when y'd 'ad a wee y'ad a shit.
MIKE: Utterly farfetched.
JANE: A know wot y' did.
MIKE: W' y' there?
JANE: Well

Silence.

Scene 67. Mike's Imagination.

MIKE: He'd be late back at the dairy.
JANE: No. He wasn't late back at the dairy.
MIKE: No?
JANE: No - He used teleportation!
MIKE: Teleportation?
JANE: He unconsciously teleported himself and the float back to her house.
MIKE: Wow!
JANE: He transmitted the float across the town. In the twinkling of an eye.
MIKE: A talent like that and he's only a milkman?
JANE: And delivered her milk.
MIKE: So Miss Smith is standing in her kitchen and suddenly the milk float appears?
JANE: Well
MIKE: It suddenly explodes into being out of thin air?
JANE: Well

MIKE: And she's not going to have a heart attack?
JANE: Well
MIKE: She's not going to remember it?
JANE: Well
MIKE: She's not going to mention it?
JANE: Well
MIKE: At least in passing?
JANE: Well

Silence.

Scene 68. Jane's Imagination.

MIKE: Did y' see wot A did?
JANE: Aye.
MIKE: Y' wot?
JANE: A did.
MIKE: 'Ow?
JANE: Y'd be surprised.
MIKE: Surprise me.
JANE: Thru t' keyoyl.
MIKE: T' keyoyl.
JANE: A w' lukkin' thru t' keyoyl
MIKE: Y' weren't
JANE: A was
MIKE: Y' can't 'a' been
JANE: 'Ow d' y' know?
MIKE: Becos I w' lukkin' thru t' keyoyl.

Silence.

Scene 69. Mike's Imagination.

JANE: Well - the milkman didn't teleport the float up
the cul-de-sac!
MIKE: Where did he teleport it to - up Miss Smith's
bustle?
JANE: She doesn't wear a bustle.

MIKE: Oh yes she does.
JANE: Bustles went out a hundred years ago.
MIKE: Not Miss Smith's. She was born with hers about sixty years ago.
JANE: He teleported it round the corner from the cul-de-sac.
MIKE: The corner?
JANE: Yes. So Miss Smith saw it approaching in the normal way.
MIKE: Normal?
JANE: Yes.
MIKE: Did I hear normal?
JANE: Yes.
MIKE: Did you say normal?
JANE: Yes.
MIKE: The normal way?
JANE: Yes.
MIKE: I thought you didn't believe in the normal.
JANE: Of course I do.
MIKE: You surprise me.
JANE: As long as it's paranormal.
MIKE: That's gibberish!
JANE: No it's not.
MIKE: The product of a woolly mind.
JANE: The product of a subtle mind.
MIKE: Oh never mind! The float approaches in a 'normal' way?
JANE: That's right.
MIKE: But it's the second time Miss Smith has seen it, it's an hour later and she's already complained!

Silence.

Scene 70. Jane's Imagination.

MIKE: Becos I w' lukkin thru t'keyoyl.
JANE: Y' want lukkin thru t' keyoyl.
MIKE: From t' opposite direction

JANE: A don't believe it.
MIKE: An A never saw you.
JANE: A lukked thru intermittently.
MIKE: Wot d' y' mean?
JANE: I oscillated
MIKE: Y' didn't
JANE: Between lukkin' thru and not lukkin' thru.
MIKE: Why shud y' do that?
JANE: So y' wun't catch me.
MIKE: Nonsense
JANE: An y' din't
MIKE: Why shud y' be lukkin' thru t' keyoyl?
JANE: Why shun't A?
MIKE: Why shud y'?
JANE: A'm a coprophiliac.
MIKE: A wot?
JANE: A coprophiliac.
MIKE: Y're not.
JANE: I am
MIKE: Y' don't know wot it meens
JANE: Course A do.
MIKE: Y' wun't know where t' begin.
JANE: Y' begin at the end.
MIKE: Don't be facetious.
JANE: A wasn't.
MIKE: Y' w're tryin' t' be.
JANE: Anyway
MIKE: Anyway wot?
JANE: Why w' you lukkin' thru?
MIKE: Lukkin' thru wot?
JANE: T' keyoyl
MIKE: Well

Silence.

Scene 71. Mike's Imagination.

JANE: Well - the milkman teleported the float back in

58

time as well as space!

MIKE: Oh yare?

JANE: Yes, he teleported it back to 8 a.m.

MIKE: Back to 8 a.m.?

JANE: Yes, and consciously forgot about the first time.

MIKE: And what about Miss Smith and the postman?

JANE: He teleported them back too.

MIKE: And they consciously forgot about the first time?

JANE: Yes.

MIKE: So they all went back to the same situation?

JANE: Yes.

MIKE: Exactly the same situation?

JANE: Exactly.

MIKE: But if it's exactly the same the milkman's not going to deliver the milk again!

JANE: Well

Silence.

Scene 72. Jane's Imagination.

MIKE: Tekkin' precautions

JANE: Precautions?

MIKE: Mekkin' sure A wasn't seen.

JANE: Seen?

MIKE: Seen doin' nowt.

JANE: Well if y' din't do owt.

MIKE: A did nothing.

JANE: Why go in?

MIKE: Ah.

JANE: Why go in at all?

MIKE: Ah

JANE: If y' wan't goin' t' do owt.

MIKE: F' show

JANE: Show?

MIKE: Show.

JANE: Wot d' y' meen?

MIKE: A front.
JANE: A front?
MIKE: T' put y' off t' scent
JANE: Off wot scent?
MIKE: 'at A wan't doin' owt.
JANE: Why din't y' want me t' know?
MIKE: Y'd 'a' tried t' stop me.
JANE: Stop y'?
MIKE: Aye stop me stoppin'
JANE: Stop y' stoppin'?
MIKE: Stop me stoppin' shittin'.
JANE: A wudn't
MIKE: Y' wud
JANE: A wun't 'a' stopped y' stoppin'
MIKE: But y'd 'a' tried t' mek me start again.
JANE: Mek y' start?
MIKE: Mek me go
JANE: Why shud A?
MIKE: Becos y' can't bear innovation.
JANE: A can.
MIKE: Y' can't.

Silence.

Scene 73. Mike's Imagination.

JANE: Well - it's not exactly the same situation.
MIKE: You just said it was.
JANE: Well I meant it's not exactly exactly.
MIKE: Well how exactly is not exactly?
JANE: Because unconsciously the milkman knows it's
        not the same. Because he's satisfied his need to
        deprive Miss Smith of her milk.
MIKE: So the milkman delivers the milk?
JANE: That's right.
MIKE: Miss Smith collects it?
JANE: Yes.
MIKE: And the postman sees her do it?

JANE: Yes.
MIKE: Then what?
JANE: They're all teleported back to an hour before.
MIKE: And their memories?
JANE: They all remember the milk being delivered.
MIKE: So everything's hunky dory?
JANE: Yes.
MIKE: Miss Smith waters her flowers and the milkman and the postman finish their rounds?
JANE: Yes.
MIKE: Then why did Miss Smith complain?
JANE: What?
MIKE: Why did she think she hadn't received her milk?
JANE: Well
MIKE: And why did the postman agree with her?
JANE: Well

Silence.

Scene 74. Jane's Imagination.

MIKE: Y' can't.
JANE: Well why 'ave y' stopped?
MIKE: Stopped what?
JANE: Stopped shittin'
MIKE: A've given it up f' Mischief Night.
JANE: F' wot?
MIKE: F' Mischief Night.
JANE: That's Lent.
MIKE: It's Mischief Night.
JANE: Lent
MIKE: It's Mischief Night.
JANE: It's Lent y' give up stuff foh.
MIKE: No.
JANE: Y' don't give up stuff foh Mischief Night.
MIKE: Well I do.
JANE: Wot foh?

MIKE: A sense of achievement.
JANE: Stoppin' shittin'?
MIKE: Summat 'at 'asn't been dun before.
JANE: 'Course it 'as.
MIKE: Wot d' y' meen?
JANE: It's been dun before.
MIKE: O' by?
JANE: Many a time.
MIKE: O' by?
JANE: Any number.
MIKE: Name one.
JANE: Right
MIKE: Cum on.
JANE: Now let me think.
MIKE: Y' can't
JANE: Aye - now - wot was 'is name?
MIKE: Wot was 'o's name?
JANE: Oh — er — y'know 'o' A meen
MIKE: A don't.
JANE: Y' do — y've 'eard of 'im — 'istorical — ee
MIKE: Cum off it.
JANE: Ee — now wot was 'is name?
MIKE: Give over
JANE: Quite famous — er
MIKE: Give over.

Silence.

Scene 75. Mike's Imagination.

JANE: Well - the milkman hadn't as much power over
their minds as he has over his own.
MIKE: What's that supposed to mean?
JANE: Well in the case of the postman the new
memory quickly faded and was replaced by the
old.
MIKE: And in the case of Miss Smith?
JANE: Well when she opened the door she felt

confused.

MIKE: I bet she did.

JANE: The second experience wasn't strong enough to suppress the first. The earlier experience and the later experience clashed in her mind. She couldn't be sure whether she could see the milk or not see the milk.

MIKE: What did the postman think of her confusion?

JANE: He didn't notice it, it only lasted a second.

MIKE: And then what?

JANE: Her unconscious mind made a compromise. She would see the milk bottles but see them as something else.

MIKE: See them as something else?

JANE: That's right.

MIKE: What did she see them as?

JANE: Her cat.

MIKE: What?

JANE: She saw them as her cat.

MIKE: Her cat?

JANE: Yes.

MIKE: She saw two milk bottles as her cat?

JANE: That's right.

MIKE: What did the postman see them as?

JANE: Milk bottles of course

MIKE: How banal of him.

JANE: Don't be

MIKE: But Miss Smith saw them as her cat?

JANE: Yes

MIKE: Not as her giraffe or piranha fish?

JANE: No!

MIKE: But as her cat?

JANE: Yes. She has a cat. We've seen it.

MIKE: True.

JANE: And cats often sit on doorsteps

MIKE: True.

JANE: Waiting to be let in.

MIKE: True.

JANE: So she could expect to see her cat on the
        doorstep.
MIKE: But she never mentioned the cat being on her
        doorstep.
JANE: Why should she? It didn't seem relevant.
MIKE: Well why wasn't her real cat there?
JANE: I don't know, on that morning it was
        somewhere else.
MIKE: Where? The British Library ?
JANE: No. Somewhere in the garden.
MIKE: So what did she do with the cat that was really
        two milk bottles?
JANE: Picked it up and took it into the kitchen.
MIKE: Where did she put it - I mean them?
JANE: On the table.
MIKE: The table?
JANE: Yes.
MIKE: But cats move about.
JANE: So?
MIKE: Bottles don't.
JANE: Well

Pause.

Scene 76. Jane's Imagination.

MIKE: Give over
JANE: Now wait a minute — A'll think of 'is name —
        er — yes!
MIKE: Give over
JANE: Jesus!
MIKE: Jesus?
JANE: Jesus
MIKE: Jesus 'o?
JANE: Y' know.
MIKE: Cud be any one a' thousands.
JANE: No, not this one
MIKE: Y' don't meen that bloke 'o used t' hang round

t' Regent Cinema?

JANE: No not 'im.

MIKE: 'E used t' shit.

JANE: A know 'e did

MIKE: All over t' seats

JANE: A sat in it once.

MIKE: 'E w' renowned for it.

JANE: 'E attracted attention.

MIKE: Sumtimes more than t' pictures they showed.

JANE: But 'is name wan't Jesus.

MIKE: It was.

JANE: T' Jesus I meen w' quite famous in 'is own right.

MIKE: 'O d' y' meen?

JANE: Christ - Jesus Christ.

MIKE: 'O?

JANE: That's 'im.

MIKE: Jesus Christ?

JANE: Aye.

MIKE: Wot about 'im?

JANE: 'E stopped.

MIKE: Stopped wot?

JANE: Stopped shittin'

MIKE: Never

JANE: 'E did

MIKE: When?

JANE: In t' wilderness

MIKE: Wot wilderness?

JANE: Forty days and forty nights

MIKE: 'E din't stop shittin'.

JANE: 'E did

MIKE: 'E stopped eatin'

JANE: It's t'same thing.

MIKE: It's not.

JANE: If y' stop eatin' y' stop shittin'

MIKE: Duzn't foller.

JANE: If nowt guz in nowt c'n cum out.

MIKE: Duzn't foller in 'is case

JANE: 'O's case?
MIKE: Jesus's case.
JANE: 'Ow d' y' meen?
MIKE: 'E cud work miracles.
JANE: 'O sez?
MIKE: 'E cud produce shit out o' nothin'
JANE: 'E cudn't.
MIKE: Cunjer it up.
JANE: A don't believe it.
MIKE: 'E cud shit wi'out eatin'.
JANE: No.
MIKE: An' I c'n eat wi'out shittin'.

Silence.

Scene 77. Mike's Imagination.

MIKE: Didn't she wonder why the cat never moved?
JANE: Well she didn't put it on the table.
MIKE: Where did she put it?
JANE: On the floor.
MIKE: The floor.
JANE: Yes, out of the way, in the cat's basket where
        she couldn't see it.
MIKE: She put the bottles in the cat's basket?
JANE: Yes.
MIKE: And then complained she hadn't received her
        milk?
JANE: That's right.
MIKE: So what about later?
JANE: Later?
MIKE: What did she ultimately do with the milk?
JANE: Well

Silence.

Scene 78. Jane's Imagination.

MIKE: An' I c'n eat wi'out shittin'!
JANE: On'y becos y're constipated.
MIKE: Y'wot?
JANE: Y're constipated
MIKE: I am not
JANE: 'Course y' are.
MIKE: A'm not.
JANE: That's why y' can't shit.
MIKE: Oh
JANE: That's why y' can't shit!

Silence.

Scene 79. Mike's Imagination.

JANE: Well - she gave the milk to the cat.
MIKE: The cat?
JANE: Yes.
MIKE: You mean she gave the milk from two bottles
        which she thought was a cat to a cat which she
        thought was two milk bottles?
JANE: No!
MIKE: She gave the cat to the cat?
JANE: No! No! She gave the milk to her real cat!
MIKE: Oh yes, her real cat.
JANE: What about her real cat?
MIKE: What happened when her real cat came into the
        house?
JANE: Well
MIKE: When it came into the kitchen?
JANE: Well
MIKE: When she saw it moving about?
JANE: Well
MIKE: Did she think it was two milk bottles moving
        about?

Silence.

Scene 80. Jane's Imagination.

MIKE: A c'n shit if A want to.
JANE: Y' can't
MIKE: 'Course A can. Any time.
JANE: Y' can't
MIKE: Any place.
JANE: Y' can't
MIKE: A can
JANE: Y' avn't been able t' shit f' five days.
MIKE: I' ave
JANE: That's why y've not been t' t' lav.
MIKE: I' ave been t' t' lav
JANE: When?
MIKE: Yesterday.
JANE: Wot time?
MIKE: About eight thirty-five
JANE: A didn't see y'
MIKE: Y' did.
JANE: A din't

Scene 81. Mike's Imagination.

JANE: No. She thought it was her real cat which had moved from its basket
MIKE: What happened when the two cats met?
JANE: What?
MIKE: What happened when the real cat met the milk bottles cat?
JANE: Well
MIKE: Did the real cat think the milk bottles were a cat?
JANE: Well
MIKE: A strange cat in its bed?
JANE: Well
MIKE: Did it try to biff em out?
JANE: Don't be

MIKE: Or did it try to bonk em?
JANE: Stop it!
MIKE: Did Miss Smith see two cats?
JANE: No.
MIKE: Did she think she'd been drinking?
JANE: No. The cats never met.
MIKE: Never met?
JANE: No, she never saw them together.
MIKE: But she must have done.
JANE: No.
MIKE: Oh come on.
JANE: No.
MIKE: The milk bottles were in the real cat's bed.
JANE: So?
MIKE: So the real cat must've taken an interest in them.
JANE: Maybe but Miss Smith never saw the two cats together.
MIKE: Why?
JANE: Because as soon as the real cat appeared the illusory cat turned back into milk bottles
MIKE: Miss Smith saw the two milk bottles?
JANE: Yes.
MIKE: Two full bottles of milk?
JANE: Yes.
MIKE: In the cat's basket?
JANE: Yes.
MIKE: Ah! but how did she explain how they got there?

Silence.

Scene 82. Jane's Imagination.

MIKE: Y' saw me go in
JANE: Well goin' in
MIKE: Y' saw me
JANE: Wot duz that prove?

MIKE: It proves t' ole thing.
JANE: It proves y' went in.
MIKE: It proves more.
JANE: It dun't prove y' did owt.
MIKE: It duz.
JANE: Y' cudn't do owt.
MIKE: A cud
JANE: Y' cudn't.
MIKE: A did
JANE: No.
MIKE: A did a lot.
JANE: Never
MIKE: A did a great deal
JANE: You 'avn't 'ad a shit f' five days.

Silence.

Scene 83. Mike's Imagination.

JANE: Er
MIKE: Ah!
JANE: Er
MIKE: You can't think up a retort can you!

Brief pause.

MIKE: At last! I've won! I've reduced you to silence!
JANE: Yes.

Silence.

Scene 84. Jane's Imagination.

MIKE: Well
JANE: You 'av'n't 'ad a shit f' five days!

Brief pause

MIKE: Well
JANE: Y' can't answer that! Can y'!

Brief pause

MIKE: No.
JANE: At last A'v' won! Y' can't cum up wi owt!
        A'v' silenced y'!

Silence.

Scene 85. Mike And Jane's Thoughts.

Mike and Jane sit.

Mike and Jane speak their thoughts.

MIKE: That's reduced her
JANE: 'im t' silence
MIKE: but only in my imaginary duologue
JANE: in me mek beleev discussion
MIKE: with her
JANE: wi' 'im.
MIKE: Yes only in
JANE: me 'ead.
MIKE: But now I've accomplished that
JANE: in me imagination
MIKE: I can entice
JANE: 'im t'speek again
MIKE: her to talk again
JANE: Cant A?
MIKE: Yes, I can but only in my imagination.

Scene 86. Mike's Imagination.

Mike and Jane move about.

MIKE: As a matter of fact — some of your —

71

concoctions — aren't altogether bad.

Brief pause.

JANE: You mean that?
MIKE: Yes, for instance that infusion of chrysanthemum - well, I rather enjoyed it.
JANE: You didn't say so at the time.
MIKE: Well, perhaps not, but I wanted you to know that I — appreciate — some of the things you do.
JANE: You appreciate them?
MIKE: Yes, I do.
JANE: Well — thanks.
MIKE: Yes I

Scene 87. Jane's Imagination.

Silence.

JANE: Ey.

Silence.

JANE: Ey.
MIKE: Wot?
JANE: Er, A'd like y' tell y' summat.
MIKE: Wot?
JANE: A think y' luk good.
MIKE: Y' don't meen that.
JANE: A do.
MIKE: Do y'?
JANE: A do. In fact
MIKE: Wot?
JANE: A lov'y'.
MIKE: Y' lov' me?
JANE: Aye. A do.
MIKE: Well — ta.

JANE: Aye A
Scene 88. Mike And Jane's Thoughts.

Mike and Jane sit.

Mike and Jane speak their thoughts.

MIKE: Yes, but I'll only be able
JANE: t' shut 'im up then open 'im up
MIKE: in reality if she
JANE: 'e speeks first.
MIKE: As I imagined her
JANE: 'im doin' in t'
MIKE: first place!

Scene 89. Mike's Imagination.

Mike and Jane move about.

JANE: You!
MIKE: Eh?
JANE: I said you!
MIKE: Me?
JANE: Yes you!
MIKE: Ah.
JANE: I've been watching you!
MIKE: Have you?
JANE: Yes. You look as though you might interest me!
MIKE: Do I?
JANE: Yes. I feel that you might amuse me.
MIKE: You feel that I might amuse you?
JANE: I do. I have a lot of intuition about such
        matters.
MIKE: Intuition.
JANE: That's right.
MIKE: I don't believe in intuition!
JANE: You don't.
MIKE: No, I think it's nonsense!

JANE: Oh.
MIKE: I think you're seriously misprised.
JANE: Oh.
MIKE: Yes, you're seriously misprised!

Scene 90. Jane's Imagination.

MIKE: Ey!

Silence.

MIKE: Ey!

Silence.

MIKE: A'm speekin t'y!
JANE: Me?
MIKE: Aye.
JANE: Why?
MIKE: A'v' bin lukkin at y'.
JANE: Lukkin at me?
MIKE: Aye. An A'll tell y summat!
JANE: Wot?
MIKE: Y' luk good!
JANE: Wot?
MIKE: Y' luk good.
JANE: Luk good?
MIKE: Aye. In fact
JANE: Wot?
MIKE: A lov'y!
JANE: Y wot?
MIKE: A lov'y!
JANE: Y wot?
MIKE: A lov'y!
JANE: Y wot?
MIKE: A sed A lov'y!
JANE: Wot d'y'meen?

Scene 91. Mike And Jane's Thoughts.

Mike and Jane sit.

Mike and Jane speak their thoughts.

MIKE: Yes, I've reached a point in my imaginary duologue with her where I've reduced her to silence in order to induce her to speak again.

JANE: 'Av 'shut 'im up then wheedled 'im in t' re-openin 'is gob.

MIKE: Yes reduce to induce. Very succinct.

JANE: Ee A'm a clever lass. I am that!

MIKE: Mm. I'm extremely adept but only

JANE: in mek beleev. Ony in me 'ead.

MIKE: Yes. I want to carry the ploy out in practice.

JANE: Say summat 'at meks 'im speechless.

MIKE: Then I'll be in the commanding position

JANE: an A c'n wheedle 'im back t'yappin.

MIKE: But she has to speak first and only then will I be able to silence her.

JANE: 'E as t'open so I c'n shut.

MIKE: She must break the silence so I can silence her.

JANE: Aye, if 'e speeks f 'starters, it'll put 'im in me power.

MIKE: Which is highly elegant.

JANE: It'll weeken 'im

MIKE: make her vulnerable

JANE: an mek 'im mine

MIKE: make her mine

JANE: So cum on lad

MIKE: Let's hear it lady!

JANE: Open y'trap!

MIKE: Stum! Will she always remain stum?

JANE: Will 'e ever say owt? Am A wastin me time?

MIKE: Is she interested in me?

JANE: Duz'e fancy me?

MIKE: Well, she
JANE: 'e stays put.
MIKE: Has she seen me looking at her?
JANE: As'e lukked at me?
MIKE: When I
JANE: wa'nt
MIKE: looking at her
JANE: lukkin at im?
MIKE: Well, there's been no direct eye-contact.
JANE: Oh no, A'v' niftily avoided that.
MIKE: But I think she
JANE: 'e most likely 'as dun.
MIKE: Yes, and she
JANE: 'e 'asnt skedaddled.
MIKE: I can't speak first!
JANE: Oh no! Bugger off that thought!
MIKE: I can't make the first move. First move of the lips.
JANE: A'v' tried that wi 'a cupple a guys
MIKE: some women I found attractive.
JANE: It meks me shudder t'think about it.
MIKE: It was a disaster from the first syllable.
JANE: A trapped meself by openin' me trap.
MIKE: They silenced me.
JANE: They slammed it shut.
MIKE: They made
JANE: me theirs.
MIKE: Oh the agony!
JANE: Oh no, dun't work!
MIKE: No, never again.
JANE: A can't win.
MIKE: I can't break the silence
JANE: then force t' silence.
MIKE: No, I'll have to wait. Maintain the silence. And bide my time!
JANE: The's nowt for it but t' ang on an' keep mum!
MIKE: Hav'n't spoken to anyone
JANE: other 'an in mek beleev

MIKE: for, oh I don't know how long.

JANE: Aye, when w't' last time?

MIKE: Apart from a large scotch please; a baguette
          please.'

JANE: Sumdy asked me directions. Me! As if I know
          where owt is. But A reckoned A did din't A.

MIKE: But this has happened before and before.

JANE: Ee'ow many times 'av' A been in this pickle
          before? Waitin' f' gobbo?

MIKE: Yes. Remember, years ago?

JANE: Huh, thinkin' back t'that summer.

MIKE: Oh yes, how could I forget it?

JANE: Oh it w'r' a byootiful summer.

MIKE: It was early spring.

JANE: A summer t'mek y'sing like a lark.

MIKE: Everything was bright, fresh, crisp, clean.

JANE: Aye, a blazin sun in a cleer blue sky, wi' nowt
          but a few milky wisps floatin'by.

MIKE: There was an intoxication in the air; I can smell
          it. Mm.

JANE: An'a balmy breeze t'keep y'eesy an' comfy, Aye.

MIKE: Everything was burgeoning. The colour of the
          flowers, sharp against the dark soil. Oh they
          brought a yelp to my heart.

JANE: Not 'at I w' singin', or eesy or comfy

MIKE: But I was yearning!

JANE: No, far from it!

MIKE: Yearning for conversation.

JANE: A'w'parched f't'lack' a' conversation.

MIKE: Any conversation! Yearning with such intensity!

JANE: Oh aye! A' w' thirsty alrite!

MIKE: Yes. And I couldn't find one, not a one,
          anywhere near where I lived.

JANE: A' w' cravin f' sumdy t' av' a natter wi'

MIKE: Then I recalled a bar.

JANE: So A thought t' meself, why not go t' t' seaside?
          Why not 'av an 'oliday from bein' on y' tod?

MIKE: yes, miles and miles away
JANE: Down by t' sea the'll be all these fellers on t 'lukkout f 'sumdy just like me.
MIKE: where I'd been only once
JANE: So A went t' t' seaside
MIKE: Can't remember why.
JANE: an' A sat in this caffy arfway down t'cliff
MIKE: But in this bar a man'd spoken to me. Spoken to me first.
JANE: wi' big winders, overlukkin' t' beach an' t' sea.
MIKE: He was a janitor
JANE: Oh it w'so nice in there
MIKE: or did he clean the streets?
JANE: wi' t' sun twinklin' an' shimmerin' on t' sea
MIKE: Something like that.
JANE: an' t' murmer a' t' waves cummin' in.
MIKE: Doesn't matter.
JANE: A cud a reely unwind meself there. Aye.
MIKE: And all he talked about were greyhounds
JANE: If I 'an' t' been so frantic about 'avin' a chat.
MIKE: of which I knew nothing
JANE: Anyway, this feller came in
MIKE: and wish to know nothing.
JANE: an' A knew at a glance 'e want my type.
MIKE: Yes, he was a boring man
JANE: No 'e w' runtish an' tanned.
MIKE: with a speech impediment
JANE: Wi' tattooz on 'is arms
MIKE: but it was an exchange of sorts.
JANE: an' rings pierced thru everything else
MIKE: He told me he was always in the bar
JANE: 'is ears, 'is lips, between 'is nostrils - oo it lukked like snot!
MIKE he was in there every evening
JANE: But surprise, surprise, 'e came over t'me an asked me if A w'r' on 'oliday.
MIKE: without exception.
JANE: Well, normally A'd' a' got shut of 'im like a shot.

MIKE: Yes, that's what he said.

JANE: But since me need t'tattle w'so urgent A let im rattle on.

MIKE: So I trekked

JANE: An' we 'ad a kind of a natter.

MIKE: and trekked is the right word

JANE: A meen 'e went on about surfin' an stuff like that, an' I can't even swim.

MIKE: all the miles and miles to the bar

JANE: T'bath at 'ome wan't big enuff

MIKE: to see him again.

JANE: Aye, it wan't much but it w' better 'an nowt an' A wanted it t' go on.

MIKE: Took me hours.

JANE: Then suddenly!

MIKE: But I got there.

JANE: Snap!

MIKE: The big moment arrived.

JANE: An 'ole gang like 'im tumbled in.

MIKE: And I went in.

JANE: Both lads an' lasses, all tattood an' pierced thru.

MIKE: He wasn't there!

JANE: An' in a flash

MIKE: After all the inconvenience!

JANE: in a trice

MIKE: He just wasn't present!

JANE: 'e turned away from me

MIKE: and I couldn't even enquire about him

JANE: t'join 'is pals!

MIKE: because I didn't even

JANE: Just like that!

MIKE: know his name!

MIKE Oh why oh why am I like this?

JANE: Ollus gagged?

MIKE: Until others are willing to speak?

JANE: Why can't A speak first an' mek meself t'gaffer?

MIKE: Other people do it and don't seem to come to any harm.

JANE: But I can't pull it off.
MIKE: No.
JANE: Why've A no pals?
MIKE: Why can't I make a relationship?
JANE: Why've A no feller? No 'usband?
MIKE: No partner? No ongoing relationship?
JANE: Oh Am so tired a bein' on me tod!
MIKE: So lonely! So alone!
JANE: A bein'in wot? In solitary! Aye!
MIKE: Oh, I - ache - with this silence!
JANE: This everlastin' nowt!
MIKE: Its excruciating!
JANE: 'Ow long c'n
MIKE: I endure it?
JANE: A'm screemin' in silence!
MIKE: I'm beseeching without sound!
JANE: Pleese reech out t' me!
MIKE: Fracture this emptiness!
JANE: A'm yowlin!
MIKE: I'm crying out!
JANE: 'Ear me! 'Ear me!
MIKE: Hear me! Hear me!
JANE: 'Ear me! 'Ear me!
MIKE: Hear me! Hear me!

Scene 92. Mike And Jane's Fantasies.

MIKE: Well, whilst I'm waiting for her to shatter the silence what shall I do to pass the time? Well, why don't I indulge in one of my favourite fantasies, yes, if not my favourite story? Yes, I don't know why I savour it, or why I find it enthralling, or why I find it comforting, but I do. Oh yes, I do. Now, how does it go?

JANE: A need summat t' do while A'm sittin' thru all this 'ush. Aye. A'll do what I ollus do when A'v' nowt else t' do. Pamper meself wi' one a me daydreams. Aye. A will. But which one? A know! That'll do nicely. Aye. A relish it don't A? It's soothin' in't it. Why? 'O the 'ell cares. But A know 'ow it begins, you bet A do.

MIKE: There was this doctor. However, he wasn't simply an ordinary physician. Oh no, he was an eminent specialist; he was an obstetrician, a consultant obstetrician, and also a gynaecologist. Yes, extremely distinguished. He was the Head of an exclusive and highly regarded In Vitro Fertilisation Unit. Mm. And the purpose of this unit was the treatment of women who wished to conceive but were hindered from doing so by defective fallopian tubes.

JANE: Anthea's loaded. Aye. Left a lot a munny by 'er dad an' mam. 'O w' kind folk. An' refined. She's well educated, lives in a mansion. In t' posh part of a city. Aye. An she 'as an 'ousekeeper t'luk after 'er.

MIKE: In the unit, eggs were removed from women and sperm was removed from their partners. These were placed together in test tubes and then deposited inside incubators, where fertilisation could occur.

JANE: Anthea lives a dazzlin' life. She's an ace racin' car driver. She's won lots a prizes. Aye. She's also a brilliant engineer. She 'as this werkshop in t' grounds of 'er 'ouse. Aye. An' when she's not werkin she's ollus snazzily dressed, an' wines an' dines at t' best restrants.

MIKE: When the eggs were fertilised, they were implanted back into their women donors, who subsequently became pregnant.

JANE: One mornin a strange packij arrives by post. T 'ousekeeper teks it t' Anthea in t' werkshop. Anthea wunders; wot the 'eck is it? She's expectin' no packij. Wot's inside?

MIKE: One day something quite wonderful happened.

Yes. An astoundingly beautiful young woman walked into the doctor's consulting room. Yes, just like that, like a spring breeze, she simply walked into his life. He was immediately entranced. Wow! So he was! But, unfortunately, oh so unfortunately, she failed to fall in love with him.

JANE: Wi' t' 'ousekeeper lukkin' over 'er shoulder, Anthea carefully opens t' packij. Wot's this? Luks like sum sort a kit. Summat t' fit together. But wot'll it be when it's all joined up? The's no note wi'it. No diagram. No instructions. Wottever it is; why shud sumdy send it to 'er?

MIKE: Who was this young woman? Well, she'd just finished her training as a missionary, and she was shortly leaving the country. There was nothing wrong with her fallopian tubes. Oh no, on the contrary, she wanted to be sterilised. She didn't want the risk of pregnancy to interfere with her mission.

JANE: Anthea's a bit wary. Cud t'thing be dangerous? Oh no, laffs t' 'ousekeeper. It luks like a toy. It must be a leg-pull from one a y'pals. If y' fit it t'gether, y'll get joke, it'll tell y' 'o sent it. Yes, sez Anthea, y'rite.

MIKE: With great sadness and reluctance the obstetrician performed the operation and sterilised the missionary. Yes he did. However, without her knowledge, he removed some of her eggs.

JANE: Anthea starts tryin' t' fit t' peeces t'gether. But by dinner time, in t' evenin', she's on'y manijed t' put sum of em t' gether. An' she still 'as no inklin' wot t' thing mite be. After dinner she guz back t' t' werkshop, an guz on playin' wi' t' mysterious contraption. T' 'ousekeeper guz back t' t' kitchen an' starts doin' t' dishes.

MIKE: The obstetrician then placed some of his own

	sperm with the missionary's eggs, in order to fertilise them. And when this was accomplished he put the eggs into special refrigeration, where they'd be preserved indefinitely. Yes. He was the Head of the unit and nobody'd find out.
JANE:	Boom! T'ousekeeper 'ears a terrific explosion! From t' direction a't' werkshop. She's 'orrified but dashes thru t'grounds. T' werkshop's a shambles. T 'doors blown off. T' winders a' shattered. Th's smashed equipment all over t'shop. Smoke an' dust fill t' air. She c'n dimly mek out Anthea, lyin' crumpled an' still. She rings for an ambulance.
MIKE:	Shortly after the operation the missionary went abroad. She abruptly vanished from the obstetrician's life. Oh it was a black day for him. He felt almost suicidal. Yes, it was as though she'd ripped herself away. Until that day he'd hoped against hope that she might stay. But now she'd gone; his love turned into hate.
JANE:	Anthea's unconscious. T' doctors aren't sure 'ow drastic 'er injuries are. T' ousekeeper, o's in a state a shock, an' blames 'erself f'r encouragin' Anthea t'mess about wi' t' contraption, is kept in 'ospital overnite.
MIKE:	The obstetrician wanted revenge! He wanted to kill the missionary! But this was impossible. She was on the other side of the world and he'd no way of finding her.
JANE:	T' next mornin' t' 'ousekeeper's told 'at Anthea's bodily injuries are on'y skin deep. But she's suffered a tremendous shock. T' doctors aren't sure if the's been any brain damage.
She's	still unconscious, an' they don't know when, or even if, she'll cum round.
MIKE:	However, the obstetrician wanted to be a

bringer of life as well as a bringer of death. Oh yes. He not only wanted to kill the missionary; he wanted to give life to her too. Mm. To resurrect her; by creating a daughter he could love and cherish. This was why he'd fertilised her eggs and frozen them.

JANE: T' cops examine t'reckij. They find part a t' contraption. They reckon it w'r a bomb. But beyond that, they get nowhere.

MIKE: The obstetrician's plan was to implant the missionary's eggs into a succession of women, until one of the women gave birth to a daughter who closely resembled the missionary.

JANE: Anthea duz come round. An slowly she starts t' remember. Skimpy stuff at first. Then more an more important stuff. But she meks mistakes. 'S on'y t' be expected, say t' doctors, 'Er mem'rys goin' t' be patchy for a long while.

MIKE: Of course, there was no guarantee the eggs would produce such a duplicate daughter. No. He'd just have to hope that they would.

JANE: Months go by. T'doctors decide Anthea's fit enuff t' go 'ome. She teks it easy. Then guz on long relaxin' cruises. Aye, very nice. T' warm an' glamorous places. In t' finish, she's completely better, an' she teks up 'er life an' career where they left off.

MIKE: And there were dangers. The children wouldn't look like their supposed parents. They'd look like the missionary or the obstetrician. Yes. What could he do?

JANE: But she never remembers owt about t' bomb or t' explosion. Nowt 'at mite 'elp t' police. Nay. T' mystr'y of 'o sent it remains. Aye, it duz that.

MIKE: The obstetrician was cunning. Mm. To avoid any risk he'd only implant eggs into women with some physical similarity to either the missionary or himself. Or conversely; into women whose partners had some physical similarity to either himself or the missionary. Thereby making it entirely plausible the children were the couple's own blood offspring. Yes.

JANE: Change a' scene. A seedy section of a dead dorp. Edith's mam and dad w' poor, Aye. An' pig ignorant. 'Er dad cud 'ardly reed an' rite. 'E w' seldom sober. 'E subdued Edith an' er mam wi' 'is brutality. Edith 'ad a drab, mis'rable existence. Ollus underfed. Shabbily dressed. Often bruised from 'er dad's beltin's. As soon as she cud she w'r off. Out a' t' road. In t' t' army.

MIKE: There mustn't be the slightest whisper that all was not as it was supposed to be.

JANE: For a cupple a' years she never went back. Never went back once. Then she thought she'd spend a few days leev there. She 'oped 'er dad mite 'a' mellowed. She met 'im in t'pub. For a bit things wan't too bad. But after a few pints 'e w' back t' badmouthin 'er. T' same as 'e'd ollus dun before. Accusin'er of owt 'e cud think of. On'y this time 'e added summat new.

MIKE: After the missionary's departure, a series of suitable couples presented themselves to the doctor.

JANE: 'E told Edith she wan't is daughter. An' is missis wan't 'er mam. Edith w'reely a twin. Aye. 'Er reel mam'd died in childbirth. 'E an' 'is missis 'd adopted 'er, t' other twin 'd gone sumwhere else. 'Is missis'd wanted a bairn but cun't 'av' one. She'd been chuffed t' tek Edith, but she'd soon cum t'rue it.

MIKE: The first woman gave birth to a son who looked like a compound of the obstetrician and the missionary.

JANE: Edith 'ad'n't credited t' tale. It w' just anuther of er dad's sozzled ramblin's. But then sum years later, when she'd been booted out t' army an' cud on'y get menial jobs, she w' watchin' t' telly.

MIKE: The second woman gave birth to a daughter who looked like a compound of the missionary and the obstetrician.

JANE: When t' news came on th' w'r a bit about car racin'. Sum woman driver'd won sum gong. When t' woman appeered on t' screen Edith neerly fell off'er chair! T' lass on t' screen w' t' spittin' imij of 'er! T' air w' dun differently but otherwise they w'r identical! This must be t' other twin'er dad 'd gone on about! T' woman on t' screen w'r Anthea. Aye, she was that. When Anthea opened er gob, even t' voice sounded similar. Except t' accent wan' t' same. Edith w'r electrified. When t' bit w' repeeted she recorded it.

MIKE: The third woman gave birth to a son whose looks rather favoured his obstetrician father.

JANE: Edith became obsessed wi' Anthea. She studied 'er. Stuff about 'er in t' papers, specially in motor racin' mags. Owt about 'er on t' box. She studied 'er voice. Aye. An' in disguise, she even went t' t' suberb where Anthea lived.

MIKE: Well, the obstetrician began to despair of ever achieving his goal. Yes, he felt extremely pessimistic. But then a fourth woman came along and gave birth to a daughter who looked astonishingly like the missionary! Yes, almost identical! The gamble had paid off!

JANE: On one of these trips, Edith spotted 'at Anthea w'r' advertisin f'r a new 'ousekeeper. Edith's parents w' both dead by this time; but she 'ad an elderly aunt she got on wi'. Edith tuk this aunt into 'er confidence. If she'd act as a spy in Anthea's mansion she'd eventually share in any spoils.

MIKE: The obstetrician had ignored his previous test-tube children. But now he had a daughter who looked so much like the missionary he took a close interest in her. Of course he did. And as she grew up with her surrogate parents, he became an intimate friend of the family.

JANE: Edith's aunt, under a false name, landed t' job of Anthea's 'ousekeeper. She cud find out stuff about Anthea 'at Edith cun't do on er own. An' she cud pinch sum samples of Anthea's 'and writin'.

MIKE: Then something cataclysmic occurred! Something completely unforeseen... When the duplicate daughter was in her twenties, the missionary returned to this country the first time since she'd gone away!

JANE: From t' aunt's reports, it w' obvious 'at neither Anthea n' nubdy 'o knew 'er, 'ad any inklin' at she w'r a twin or 'd been adopted.

MIKE: One day, shortly after her arrival, the missionary was walking down the street. When suddenly! Quite by accident. Wham! She came face to face with the obstetrician!

JANE: Edith'd lernt 'ow t'mek bombs in t' army. An' she knew 'at Anthea w'r' a clever engineer. She designed an bilt a bomb 'at seemed like a toy. Aye. An then she dismantled it. She sent it t' Anthea 'opin' it'd luk 'armless an appeel t' Anthea's curiosity. An', in fact, it w'r' 'armless, becos it 'ad no detonator.

MIKE: But she didn't recognise him until he spoke to her. She'd never even thought about him in the years she'd been away. Why should she? What 'd been a deeply disturbing relationship for him 'd been no more than a fleeting professional transaction for her.

JANE: T' aunt, posin as t'ousekeeper, w'r' on 'and when t' bomb arrived. She w' there t' lull any suspicions Anthea mite 'av' an' t' prod 'er in t' tryin' t' put it t'gether.

MIKE: He was shocked! Confounded! But he managed to hide it. He and she chatted politely then went their separate ways.

JANE: After dinner, that evenin', Edith rang t' werkshop an' spoke t' Anthea. Aye. She sed, y' don't know 'o I am, but if y' want t' know 'o sent y' t' packij, y' must cum an' meet me now! Anthea left t' werkshop pronto!

MIKE: For her the chance encounter was merely another triviality to be easily forgotten. But for him it was excruciating! Unbearable! Ugh! All his old feelings of rage and vengeance were revived. They churned away inside him. And he desperately needed to assuage them.

JANE: T' rendivoo w'r' a bildin site. As soon as Anthea clapped eyes on Edith she w' dumbstruck. She cun't beleev it. She w' seein' 'er dubble.

MIKE: However, killing the missionary 'd no longer satisfy his vengeful feelings. No. She was too old and her appearance had changed.

JANE: As Anthea gawped, Edith tuk out an 'ammer an' crashed it down on Anthea's 'ead. Anthea w'r' an engineer an' Edith w' goin t' use engineer's tools t' kill 'er.

MIKE: The obstetrician's thoughts turned towards his daughter. She was the same age as the missionary'd been when she went away. She now looked like the missionary'd looked all those years before. His love for his daughter turned into hate. Yes. He'd exact his required revenge upon his daughter!

JANE: Anthea dropped t' t' dirt. Edith gave 'er 'ead anuther woppin' blow. Shatterin'er skull. Smitin' t' life out of 'er. Then Edith dragged Anthea's body in t' t' darkness a t' new bildin's foundations.

MIKE: Yes. But before the revenge, there was something else he had to do. Remove the surrogate parents. They might be dangerous. They connected him to the girl. Mm. He arranged for them to die in a car crash.

JANE Edith renched off Anthea's outer cloze. 'Er coat, 'er blouse, 'er designer jeans, an' 'er shoes. Then she shoved up Anthea's bra an' bared 'er tits, an' yanked down Anthea's pants an' bared 'er cunt.

MIKE: He was now ready to kill his daughter. He disguised himself, and under a false name, booked a room in a cheap hotel. He phoned his daughter and asked her to come over. As soon as she opened the door he asphyxiated her, and then stripped off her clothes. He also stripped off his own clothes so they wouldn't become bloodstained.

JANE: Then in a frenzy, Edith rained down twenty eight slashin' stabbin' chops t' Anthea's body, wi' a ten inch screwdriver sharpened to a jagged point.

MIKE: He lay his daughter on the bed, and then using a variety of scalpels and other surgical instruments, he proceeded to dismember her. He sliced through her carotid artery, almost severing her head, cutting through the neck to the vertebrae. He then spread her legs apart, exposing her pudenda; and stripped away the flesh from the abdomen and thighs, from the costal arch to the pubes. He then detached this flesh in three large flaps and piled them on a table nearby.

JANE: Edith ripped t' screwdriver in t' Anthea's tits, 'er thighs, 'er belly — rippin' it so badly 'at 'er guts spilled out. Then she ripped it in t' Antheas cunt an' punctured 'er womb.

MIKE: The obstetrician washed himself at the sink in the corner of the room, put his clothes back on, and without being noticed, slipped out of the hotel.

JANE: Edith 'd 'it t' jackpot! She'd won t' big prize! Oh aye, she 'ad that. She'd been poor an' downtrodden all 'er life while Anthea 'd been rich an' lukked up to. Fate 'd doled out almost nowt t' one twin an' dished up almost everything else t' t' other. If Fate dun't give y' y' fair share a luck then y' must give it t' y'self. That's wot Edith'd dun. Aye, wi' a vengeance. Given 'erself 'er riteful share a t' luck. Anthea wan't t' be pitied. No. Both twins 'd been about arfway thru life when she w' bumped off. Edith 'd on'y tekken arf of er' share. Arf of Anthea's life. That's rite.

MIKE: He'd been smart. Very smart. He'd taken every precaution. Yes he had. There was nothing to connect him to the victim. He'd committed that rare thing the perfect murder. Mm. A murder which became extremely notorious and extremely celebrated. Oh yes, very much so. A murder which drew much of its notoriety and much of its celebrity, from the uncontestable fact that it remained unsolved. Unsolved. Yes. Forever.

JANE: But the w'r' a lot more t' wot Edith'd dun 'an that. Oh, she'd been very sharp. She'd killed Anthea an' then sh'ad brought 'er back t' life. Aye. She'd given birth t' Anthea. She'd resurrected Anthea. She'd dun it by replacin' Anthea. By becoming Anthea. By tekkin on Anthea's glitterin' life. Now she was Anthea. Oh aye; she woh. An Anthea w' very much alive!

MIKE: Yes, that's how my fantasy goes. Of course it's only a fantasy, that's all. But I enjoy it don't I?

Yes I do!

JANE: Aye. There's me daydreem. Aye. But it dun't meen owt duz it? No. A just daydreem, dreem, dreem, an' as A do so, A purr, purr, purr.

Scene 93. Mike And Jane's Thoughts

MIKE: Well I'll never know what's possible
JANE: til A try or 'e tries
MIKE: until one of us speaks to the other.
JANE: If A speek first e'll
MIKE: she'll probably silence me
JANE: an' after that
MIKE: who knows what she
JANE: 'e mite do?
MIKE: And if she
JANE: 'e speeks first
MIKE: I'll probably silence her
JANE: silence 'im
MIKE: and after that
JANE: 'o knows
MIKE: what I
JANE: wot A mite do?
MIKE: And what else is there
JANE: except winnin' or losin?
MIKE: Well
JANE: A suppose
MIKE: We might draw

Scene 94. Mike's Imagination.

Mike and Jane move about the stage.

MIKE: So you believe in reincarnation?
JANE: A do.
MIKE: Why's that?
JANE: Becos A'm a reincarnation meself!
MIKE: Who did you used to be?

JANE: Evita.
MIKE: Eva Peron?
JANE: That's 'er.
MIKE: How do you know you were Eva Peron?
JANE: A c'n remember when A w'r' 'er.
MIKE: What can you remember?
JANE: Standin on a balcony an' oratin'
MIKE: Orating?
JANE: Aye, t' t' crowds, t' t' workers.
MIKE: Really.
JANE: Aye, an' they w'r' all bare t' t' waist.
MIKE: Bare to the waist?
JANE: Stripped t' t' waist.
MIKE: Why was that?
JANE: Becos they w' t' shirtless ones.
MIKE: Oh, los descamisados.
JANE: Aye.
MIKE: But the name doesn't literally mean they had no
        shirts.
JANE: Course it duz.
MIKE: No it's a metaphor for their poverty.
JANE: No.
MIKE: I've seen newsreels of Evita addressing the
        crowds and they're all wearing shirts.
JANE: Well
MIKE: I mean there's the evidence for all to see.
JANE: Well

Scene 95. Jane's Imagination.

JANE: Can y' write?
MIKE: Oh yes I can write quite fluently.
JANE: Wot av' y' written?
MIKE: A great many things.
JANE: Such as?
MIKE: The Origin Of Species.
JANE: Y' never.
MIKE: The Double Helix.

JANE: Y' never.
MIKE: A Brief History Of Time.
JANE: Y' never wrote them!
MIKE: What makes you say that?
JANE: Becos they w'r' all written by sumdy else.
MIKE: Oh they may have been initially written by other people but then I completely rewrote them.
JANE: 'Ow d'y meen?
MIKE: I took the books, a pen and a piece of paper and then I wrote.
JANE: Y' meen y' copied!
MIKE: Oh no, much more than that!
JANE: 'Ow cum?
MIKE: I employed the same physical means, the same movements of the wrist, fingers and pen, the previous writers had employed.
JANE: Ah!
MIKE: In short; I wrote.
JANE: Ah! But wot if they din't use a pen?
MIKE. Well
JANE: They mite a dictated, or used a typewriter, or a word processor!
MIKE: Well
JANE: Which meens at all you did w't' copy out by 'and wot w'r' in t' books!
MIKE: Well

Scene 96. Mike's Imagination.

JANE: T' newsreels are all you c'n see!
MIKE: They're what everybody can see!
JANE: They're not wot I can see!
MIKE: What are you saying?
JANE: They're nowt but an outsiders view.
MIKE: An outsiders view?
JANE: Nubdy but me as Evita knows wot A saw.
MIKE: What does that mean?

JANE: I was Evita. Its not wot I saw!
MIKE: What you saw?
JANE: Nubdy except me as Evita knows wot I saw!
MIKE: Well

Scene 97. Jane's Imagination.

MIKE: I doubt that you've ever copied anything out.
JANE: Oh yes I av'.
MIKE: Nothing of any substance.
JANE: Oh yes I 'av'.
MIKE: Pray tell me what?
JANE: The Basic Elements Of Sewage Treatment.
MIKE: Where would you copy that?
JANE: At school.
MIKE: What kind of school 'd have that on its
curriculum?
JANE: T' school A went t'
MIKE: I don't believe you.
JANE: A c'n still repeat it word for word.
MIKE: Give me a sample.
JANE: 'It's always necessary t' ensure 'at raw sewage
is reduced by degrees into a uniform sludge
which'll enable it t' be suitably distributed
amongst the sludge lagoons.'
MIKE: You could 've invented that.
JANE: No a cun't.
MIKE: Why not?
JANE: Am too stupid!

Silence.

Scene 98. Mike's Imagination.

JANE: I saw t' crowds wi' out any shirts on at all!
MIKE: Oh
JANE: Y' can't argue wi' that!
MIKE: Oh

JANE: Can't gainsay that!
MIKE: Oh but I can, what about

Scene 99. Jane's Imagination.

MIKE: No, you're not too stupid.
JANE: I am.
MIKE: No, no.
JANE: Y'v' sed so y' self!
MIKE: Well
JANE: A cun't mek up stuff like that.
MIKE: Well
JANE: Cud A?
MIKE: Alright, you may not've invented it, but you
        could've been able to

Scene 100. Mike And Jane's Thoughts.

Mike and Jane sit.

MIKE: Oh a draw could
JANE: drag on forever!
MIKE: But I've got to
JANE: do summat
MIKE: to end this agonising silence!
JANE: But if A do
MIKE: speak first
JANE: can A do owt
MIKE: to minimise the risks?
JANE: Well
MIKE: Well
JANE: Why don't A
MIKE: probe?
JANE: Aye
MIKE: probe?
JANE: That's a good idea
MIKE: why didn't I think of it before?
JANE: Aye, not cum on strong

MIKE: not commit myself
JANE: no
MIKE: but explore
JANE: feel me way
MIKE: and try to discover
JANE: suss out
MIKE: what makes her
JANE: 'im tick
MIKE: what she's like
JANE: wot 'es after.
MIKE: Yes, and if I probe she'll
JANE: 'e'll probbly probe wi'me.
MIKE: Yes.
JANE: Aye.
MIKE: Probe!

Scene 101. Mike:

MIKE: Er... excuse me.
JANE: Eh?
MIKE: Have you got the time please?
JANE: Oh... t' time.
MIKE: Yes.
JANE: Er... aye.

She looks at her watch.

It's just after five o'clock.

MIKE: After five.
JANE: Aye.
MIKE: Thankyou.
JANE: Oh that's...
MIKE: ...Ha, I forgot to put my watch on.
JANE: Oh... 'seesily dun.
MIKE: Yes.
JANE: ...A sumtimes f'get mine.
MIKE: Do you... yes... I suppose most...

JANE: Aye. A suppose so...
MIKE: Yes. I always like to have a rough idea of the
       time.
JANE: Oh aye... so do I.
MIKE: ...But usually there's a clock somewhere
       nearby... wherever you are.
JANE: ...Oh aye... or y' c'n ollus ask sumdy
MIKE: As I
JANE: As you
MIKE: As I did.
JANE: Aye.
MIKE: Ha.
JANE: ...Tho' Av been in sum places where the w' no
       clock at all.
MIKE: Oh so have I.
JANE: Aye.
MIKE: Yes.

Scene 102. Jane:

JANE: Excuse me er... can y tell me if the's a music
       shop neerby?
MIKE: A music shop.
JANE: Aye.
MIKE: Yes... yes, I believe there is.
JANE: Oh.
MIKE: Not far away
JANE: Oh.
MIKE: in that direction.
JANE: Oh.
MIKE: Yes.
JANE: ...Well that's useful t' know.
MIKE: Yes I er...
JANE: A'm thinkin about gettin' sum CDs.
MIKE: Are you?
JANE: Aye... but not, y' know, immediately.
MIKE: No.
JANE: No.

97

MIKE: No.
MIKE: You mean...
JANE: Sumtime.
MIKE   ...Yes.
JANE: Aye.
JANE: D' you ever buy...
MIKE: Oh yes, I have quite a
JANE: Aye.
MIKE: Yes I often um...
JANE: Wot sort a music...
MIKE: Do I like?
JANE: Aye.
MIKE: Well... all sorts of things...
JANE: Aye.
MIKE: Y' know...
JANE: Aye.
MIKE: Mm... what sort of
JANE: Oh... all' sorts a' stuff

Scene 103. Mike And Jane's Thoughts.

Mike and Jane speak their thoughts.

MIKE: Dare I?
JANE: 'Av'A t' guts t' do it?
MIKE: Yes, that's the crux of the problem!
JANE: Aye, that's wot it boils down t'!
MIKE: Dare I?
JANE: 'Av' t' guts?
MIKE: Dare I actually start probing?
JANE: 'Av' A t' nerve t' reelly begin probin?

Scene 104.

MIKE   Yes.
JANE: Aye.
MIKE: Do you do the lottery?

JANE: Oh aye... t' lottery.
MIKE: I like to do the lottery
JANE: Aye.
MIKE: Only a pound a week or maybe two sometimes.
JANE: Oh, on'y a quid or two.
MIKE: Yes
JANE: Aye.
MIKE: But however much... it's important to play the
         lottery.
JANE: Oh aye, it is.
MIKE: Yes.
JANE: Aye... just t' be in there.
MIKE: In with a chance.
JANE: That's rite.
MIKE: ...If you won, what would you
JANE: Wot'd A do?

They begin to lower their voices until they are speaking
silently.

MIKE: Yes
JANE: Well... A don't know
MIKE: Yeh?
JANE: A meen wot wud you
MIKE: Well I don't know
JANE: ...No?
MIKE: No.
JANE: Well...
MIKE: I might... I might...
JANE: Aye?
MIKE: I mean... what?
JANE: Well... I mite
MIKE: Yes

JANE: } Y' know
MIKE: } Yes

JANE: } A mite
MIKE: } I might.

They both freeze.

Then they stand up.

They bow to each other.

They bow to the audience.

And they walk off the stage.